And Drink I Did

One Man's Story of Growing Through Recovery

Foreword

I first published this book in 2015.

I wrote it quickly, almost hastily.

All I cared about was getting it out there, and it showed.

The story was real and true and raw, and I didn't hold any punches, but looking back, there were entire sections that should've been rewritten.

I cringed every time I read it.

The book was in desperate need of an upgrade.

I wasn't hard on myself, as most writers are.

I'm sure most of them wish they could go back and rewrite almost everything they've ever written.

But this was different.

I was lazy. And I knew it.

That was unacceptable to me. That *is* unacceptable to me.

And it's a disservice (and disrespectful) to all the other writers out there.

So I spent a few months, going back through it, one page at a time, cutting here and adding there.

I think it flows better now.

And because the original manuscript was published three years ago (and written four years ago), I've added quite a bit, with a particular emphasis on how important it is to stay active in recovery today, no matter how much time has passed.

Quite a bit has happened since then, but my story is still the same.

Like I said in the first edition, it's not particularly unique (and it may be boring to some) but it is what it is.

It's the story of my alcoholism, and it's the story of everything I lost along the way, including my sanity.

But more importantly, *most* importantly, it's a story of redemption.

And it's a story of hope.

For the sick and suffering still out there,
including my baby brother.

Prologue

Some people say they don't remember their first drink.

I'll never forget mine.

It was a six-pack of Miller Lite.

Three friends and I split a case when we were fifteen, bought for us by one said friend's older brother.

We sat around his kitchen table, playing drinking games, thinking we were the shit, and getting obliterated in the process.

I liked all of it right from the start-the fuzz, the taste, the coldness.

Then came the feeling.

I was relaxed, chill.

I felt like a million bucks-smooth, funny, good looking.

After we finished, we walked to a local dance and although I don't remember much of the walk other than a friend throwing up with such incredible velocity that the rest of us had to jump back, I do remember seeing one of the prettiest girls in town at the dance.

I remember walking up and talking to her.

She talked back. And smiled.

And that was it.

That was all it took.

I fell in love right then.

It was a love affair that would span for over twenty years, a love affair that lasted longer than any in my life.

On that chilly September night in 1987, as I stood there grinning stupidly at a pretty girl and thinking I was the coolest person in the world, I fell in love with alcohol.

PART 1: Cocktail Hour

Outside in the backyard, one of the dogs began to bark. The leaves of the aspen that leaned against the window ticked against the glass. The afternoon sun was like a presence in the room, the spacious light of ease and generosity. We could have been anywhere, somewhere enchanted. We raised our glasses again and grinned at each other like children who agreed on something forbidden.

-Raymond Carver

Chapter 1

Why am I an alcoholic?

I don't know.

What made me an alcoholic?

I don't know that either.

It doesn't matter.

What matters is that I *am* an alcoholic.

I grew up in the suburbs of Boston, about nine miles south, in a town called Braintree.

Both of my parents grew up in Dorchester, one of the many neighborhoods that make up Boston.

Neither of them is an alcoholic. Nor is anyone in their respective families.

Dad is Irish, and mom is Italian, and they moved to Braintree in 1964.

My sister Kelli was born in 1965. Andrea came along in 1966, myself in 1973, and Brian in 1974.

I had two parents who provided me with everything I needed.

We lived in a nice neighborhood in a nice house with nice neighbors. I was a better than average student and had several close friends, but I was a bit on the shy side.

I was raised with manners and dad says all four of us were very well behaved.

There is nothing in particular that stands out as far as *the* defining moment of what made me an alcoholic.

I just loved what alcohol did for me.

It got me out of myself. It let my inhibitions down.

So I drank.

A lot.

———————————

The earliest known sign of when I knew something was a little off-kilter about me was when I was eight years old, long before I ever took a sip of alcohol.

I didn't see my dad much because he was always working.

Brian and I would go to the YMCA with him on Sundays, and when we were at our cottage on Lake Winnispesaukee in New Hampshire, we were his shadow.

He still jokes that if he stopped short, both

of us would bump our little heads into his butt because we were always so close behind.

But that was the extent of us seeing him.

He was gone when we got up in the morning, and by the time he got home at night, we were already in bed.

Right after my parents separated, I remember walking to school one morning when suddenly my lunch bag broke open, spilling everything on the ground.

I freaked.

I don't know why and I still can't explain it, but I felt like the world was coming to an end.

I started hyperventilating. My palms were sweaty. I got dizzy and couldn't form a rational thought in my head.

I just stood there, staring at my sandwich and crackers, and not having any idea what to do.

Then I started to cry.

I felt so helpless.

I was completely paralyzed with fear.

Do I grab the stuff on the ground? Do I leave it? Nope, that'd be littering, and I can't litter. Am I going to be late? Do I have time to run home and get a new lunch? Will Mom be mad? Will Mike? He's waiting for me at his house. Why can't I move? Why are my feet glued to the ground? Now I'm going to be late for school. That's not good. My house is right there, I can see it, but why does it look and feel like it's a million miles away?

That entire thought process probably lasted a half a second in reality, but my mind dragged it out for what felt like an eternity.

It became a series of anxious, bombastic thoughts that were firing at such a rapid rate it felt as if my head was going to explode.

I grabbed what I could and ran home, crying and screaming as I burst through the kitchen door.

I don't remember much else.

I don't remember my mom calming me down. I don't remember going to school that day.

What I *do* remember is wanting my dad there.

I wanted him to help me, to protect me, to pick up my scattered lunch and frantic body and carry me home.

But he wasn't.

The first signs of obsessive-compulsive disorder appeared a few weeks later.

The definition:

"Obsessive-compulsive disorder (OCD) is an anxiety disorder in which people have unwanted and repeated thoughts, feelings, ideas, sensations (obsessions), or behaviors that make them feel driven to do something (compulsions). Often the person carries out the behaviors to get rid of the obsessive thoughts, but this only provides temporary relief. Not performing the obsessive rituals can cause great anxiety. A person's level of OCD can be anywhere from mild to severe, but if severe and left untreated, it can destroy a person's capacity to function at work, at school or even to lead an uncomfortable existence in the home."

I was never technically diagnosed with OCD, but I learned years later that I had it.

It started with small things that nobody noticed.

Except for me.

I noticed.

I didn't feel right or complete until I had done specific tasks.

Even after I did them, there was still a lingering sense that something was off.

When people ask me to describe it, the best I can do is to say it's like an itch that can't be scratched-kind of like when the top of your mouth tickles, and you use your tongue to scratch it, but it doesn't really help because your tongue just isn't the right instrument to scratch an itch.

It's like that.

Kind of.

It started with my kitchen ritual.

We had these drawers in the kitchen by the fridge and every morning before I left for school, I had to tap each drawer (top left, top right, followed by the others in descending order). Then I had to jump in the air.

If I didn't tap them right or if I didn't jump high enough, I'd have to do it again. And if the landing wasn't right, I'd have to do it again.

That was the first occurrence I can remember, and although it was never anything insanely crazy, my little rituals offered temporary relief, just like the definition states.

I watched an HBO documentary years later on the subject, and some people couldn't do *anything* until their compulsions were met. They ended up losing jobs, their homes, and relationships because of it.

One guy spent hours tying his shoelaces

in the morning.

By the time he tied them to his liking, he'd be hours late for work.

Another guy couldn't leave his condo complex until he had driven over a speed bump *precisely* the way he thought he should.

He lost his job (and most of his friends) because of it.

I wasn't that extreme, but I remember getting restless just watching the documentary.

I could relate.

Everything had to be in control, and I had to be the one to control it.

Soon my kitchen ritual wasn't enough.

I needed more.

So I started cleaning.

A lot.

Our house at 51 Staten Road was *the* house.

We had the type of house where the entire neighborhood hung out.

There was always at least two or three people hanging around (sometimes when none of us were home) and there were countless times when mom would wake up to several couches occupied by sleeping friends who weren't getting along with their parents or were just too tired to go home.

She never once complained about it.

But I'll never forget the day a new friend walked in and said, "Why is your house always so messy?"

I was astounded.

I didn't know what to say.

I was so caught off guard I didn't say anything. But I was embarrassed.

Our house was never dirty.

Sometimes it was messy but never dirty.

Mom was working the night shift, and between raising four children and the myriad of kids who were always over, of course, it'd be messy from time to time.

But when that kid pointed it out, I was floored.

So I started cleaning the house.

It became a necessity for me to get rid of any clutter.

And if there were too much clutter or clutter I shouldn't be touching (like mom's bills), I'd stack them into neat little piles.

My mom's spoon (complete with coffee stain) that she'd leave on the counter would drive me nuts.

Spoon in the dishwasher, wipe the coffee stain away, clean the rest of the counters with Windex, sweep the floor, make sure the sink was empty (and Soft Scrub applied), and then out came the vacuum.

I always saved the best for last.

I sensed the vacuuming was a little odd.

It wasn't the fact that I vacuumed.

All of my mom's friends thought it was the greatest thing in the world.

The thing that bothered me was that I would hide it, just like years later, when I would hide my drinking.

I didn't want it to bother anyone.

If no one were home, I'd be all set.

If someone *was,* I could still get away with all the other stuff, but I'd have to hold off on the vacuuming. That would sometimes be an issue.

I'd go off and do something else. Maybe I'd do homework or watch TV for a while, but that lingering itch would always be there, begging to be scratched.

And it would get worse.

When I'd finally be able to get to it, I felt better, at least temporarily.

The itch was scratched.

I remember my mom traveling quite a bit when I was seventeen and eighteen, and she left Brian and I home alone, complete with her car.

It was awesome.

It was like we were adults.

It was our house and would be for the next week or so.

When she left, I would spend the first day cleaning.

The counters had to be spotless. All the clutter was hidden away in drawers or closets. Candles were lit. Windows were opened to allow fresh air in.

But the funny thing was that I didn't have people over when she was gone.

Once in a while, I did, but I loved the fact that when I went out and came back home again, the house would be picture-perfect.

Of course, I still went from room to room checking to make sure. And I may have applied more Windex to the counters or swept the floors again.

But it made me feel better.

Everything was safe.

Everything was in its place.

I could relax a bit.

———————————

During the divorce, dad would visit us on Tuesdays, Thursdays and every other Sunday for the day during the school year.

In the summer we'd spend weekends and a few weeks at the lake.

My sisters were older and were either working an after-school job or out with friends when dad would come by on Tuesdays and Thursdays.

He'd sit with Brian and me as we did our homework or maybe watch TV with us for a while. Then he'd put us to bed and take turns lying with each of us as we drifted off to sleep.

It usually worked.

But one night I couldn't sleep, and I knew he was probably ready to leave (he'd been laying with me for twenty minutes or so), so I faked I was asleep.

As he got out of bed, I felt an undeniable and powerful sense of abandonment.

My dad, who had lived with us forever, was walking out of our house, at night, to some shitty, little studio apartment while his kids lay in their beds, with nothing to protect them in case something terrible happened.

He was leaving.

I heard the back door open, and as he started down the back steps, I jumped out of bed and ran after him, screaming for him to come back.

I think I scared the hell out of him because I wasn't a dramatic kid.

I jumped into his arms and screamed, "Don't leave dad. Don't leave."

It's evident I didn't mean just right then.

I meant, *Don't leave us. Ever.*

Again I had that sense that everything was entirely out of control.

And I hated it.

I hated feeling like that.

I hated not being in control.

I hated things not being in order.

I hated my dad for walking out on us.

On the day my dad told Brian and me that he and mom were getting a divorce, he sat us on his bed and told us he wasn't going to be living with us anymore, that he and mom were not going to be married anymore.

I don't remember anything beyond that because it was the first time I saw my dad cry. He hid it well and didn't completely break down, but when his eyes started watering, I was more confused than anything else.

And the enormity of the divorce didn't hit me until that night a few months later when he walked out the back door.

I never felt more alone.

Chapter 2

The Mayo Clinic defines the causes of alcoholism as the following:

"-Alcoholism is influenced by genetic, psychological, social and environmental factors that have an impact on how it affects your body and behavior.

"-The process of becoming addicted to alcohol occurs gradually, although some people have an abnormal response to alcohol from the time they start drinking. Over time, drinking too much may change the normal balance of chemicals and nerve tracks in your brain associated with the experience of pleasure, judgment and the ability to exercise control over your behavior. This may result in your craving alcohol to restore good feelings or remove negative ones."

I don't think my alcoholism is genetic.

Before me, there is no history of alcoholism in my family.

Psychological?

Who knows.

There is no history of psychological illness in my family either.

I had a great family, everything I needed and

wanted, went to a good school and grew up in an upper-middle-class neighborhood.

I was never abused, beaten, molested or even made fun of.

I was, however, sensitive.

Mom always told me I was a very secure child. She said I never needed attention, wasn't needy and could spend hours by myself.

I was just content to be alone and quiet.

When someone was obnoxious or loud, however, I would retreat further into myself, and it would take that much more for me to come out of my shell.

In seventh grade, a friend and I were in Ms. Walker's art class, sitting with two girls, joking around and flirting (or whatever can be constituted as flirting to an eleven-year-old).

I'll never forget it.

I was having a blast.

We were talking to girls, and they were talking back. And they were both cute.

I was on top of the world.

Then, out of nowhere, one of them said, "Jay, why do you have tits?"

I was crushed.

Who says that kind of thing? Who could be

so cruel?

I thought this girl liked me.

And I thought I was being ridiculously charming.

I looked down, and she was right.

I had boobs.

It didn't help that the shirt I was wearing was too small nor did it help that it wasn't a real Izod.

It was the fake kind, the one with the hippo on it, instead of the little alligator.

I instantly hated my mother for that.

I had to blame someone and blaming anyone other than myself was something I'd become an expert at as my alcoholism escalated.

Why the fuck did I have this generic Izod on? Why was it too small?

That's why it looked like I had tits.

If it were a real Izod, it wouldn't fit like this.

And instantly, one of my greatest insecurities was born.

I hated my body.

I hated my man boobs. I hated feeling like I could never take my shirt off in front of a mirror again, never mind in front of someone else, especially a girl.

One night I went to hug and kiss my dad goodbye ,and he put up his hand and said, "You're thirteen now, no more hugs and kisses. From now on we shake hands."

I've never been an affectionate person unless it's with my significant other.

I'm not a touchy-feely person and can't stand it when people touch me.

I remember when I was about nine, and we were getting ice cream at the lake with another dad and his son, and as we were walking back to the boat, the son (not the dad, but the son) put his arm around his dad's waist and the dad put his arm around his son's shoulders.

They fit together perfectly.

I was astonished.

It was so sweet and touching.

And it was something I needed and wanted from my dad.

But Dad just didn't know how to do that.

I think the reason it was a defining moment in my life was that as a little kid, my brother and I were my dad's shadow.

We were always sitting in his lap, climbing all over him, and fighting over who would get to be on his shoulders when we went for a walk.

My dad was our hero.

He had the world's biggest back, and one of my fondest memories was when Brian and I would wrap our little hands around his neck, climb on his back, and he'd swim both of us out to our swim raft.

It was like we had our own private dolphin.

We'd just hang on tight, and he'd take us where we wanted to go.

So to have that kind of affection so suddenly turned off was more confusing than anything else.

I felt I did something wrong.

What gives? What the hell did I do?

Later, when I was married and my wife had three kids of her own, I was the same way.

I could be affectionate if the kids initiated it, but I'd never do it on my own.

I think it made it a little easier because her two oldest were girls and Liz, the middle child, was super affectionate.

Now I need to say, unequivocally, without a shadow of a doubt, that I'm not blaming any of these "defining" moments on my alcoholism.

I felt a loss of control and normalcy when my lunch fell to the ground.

I felt abandoned when my dad left my bunk bed that night.

I know kids can be cruel and insensitive, as I witnessed that day in art class.

I also know my dad wasn't purposely trying to hurt me when he said we couldn't hug anymore. I know that's the way he was raised and that he was doing the best he could.

But what I *am* saying is that these events and countless more, added up to make me an insecure, confused and scared teenager.

I just didn't fit in.

I was always on the perimeter.

I was boringly handsome.

I was one of the two middle kids in the family.

I was a tiny bit better than average as a student and an average athlete.

I was well-liked amongst my peers, but girls only considered me "friend" material.

I always felt lost, but it was never anything as extreme as feeling invisible. I almost wished I was invisible because then I could just disappear.

But I always felt like people were talking about me or judging me.

I felt a void and had no idea how to fill it.

Alcohol filled that void perfectly.

It took me out of myself.

I could relax.

I knew people weren't talking about me when I drank.

I was just the quiet, good-natured guy in the corner, who was always polite and who sometimes had a tendency to smile just a bit broader when he drank.

Alcohol quelled the OCD too.

I didn't clean when I was drunk.

It didn't bother me that things weren't in their place.

I didn't sweat the small stuff, so to speak.

And I knew I wasn't sweating it. That was the beauty of it.

I *loved* not having that itch clawing at me in the back of my mind.

I remember one morning when I was living by myself in Quincy.

It was after a particularly crazy night.

I woke up hungover as hell and had the brilliant idea that I was going to stop being so neat, that I was going to beat my OCD.

I threw a T-shirt in the corner of my room.

But it didn't land right. It didn't look messy enough. So I picked it up and then threw it in the corner again.

Nope, didn't work that time either.

I spent the next two hours zipping around my apartment trying to make it look messy or at least "lived-in," rather than like a museum.

Then I left because I knew if I didn't, I'd spend the rest of the day obsessing.

I came home later that day and put everything back in its place.

Then I got drunk.

That's how my mind worked.

I was either dwelling on the past, thinking about the future, or obsessing about any number of things.

I was never in the now. I was never present.

When I drank, it pushed all the emotions aside.

I didn't worry about anything.

I was slowly slipping into oblivion and loving every minute of it.

I was never an angry drunk.

I didn't get belligerent. I didn't get sappy or emotional. I just felt relaxed.

I never looked or acted drunk either.

I didn't slur my words, didn't get sloppy, and nothing about my physical appearance changed other than I'd have a goofy grin on my face.

There were only two or three people who knew when I was drinking.

That can be a dangerous thing for a drunk because I didn't have to hide anything or try to act sober.

But in hindsight, it was just another reason why it took me so long to stop drinking.

I've had people ask me why or when or how I became an alcoholic.

I have no idea.

Does it matter?

As I said, I *am* one.

That's what matters.

I have this infliction or illness or disorder, or whatever the fuck it's being classified as now, and I know I can't drink in safety.

I'll never be cured, and it'll never go away.

And it's something I just have to live with.

Part II: The Party

Maybe we were a little drunk by then. I know it was
hard keeping things in focus. The light was draining
out of the room, going back through the window
where it had come from. Yet nobody made a move to
get up from the table to turn on the overhead light.

~Raymond Carver

Chapter 3

Tom, Greg, Steve and I were inseparable as kids.

Our neighborhood had over thirty kids between the ages of seven and seventeen, all living in an eight-block radius.

We'd be outside playing from early morning until the street lights came on.

My first experience with alcohol was when Greg knocked on my door and told me that Cliff, a much older kid, was drunk in the woods.

I ran out the back door, and by the time Greg and I got there, seven or eight other kids watching the spectacle.

The first thing I noticed was that Cliff couldn't stand up straight.

He'd try to stand, then he'd sit, then he'd try to stand again, but he'd be hunched over, and then he'd sway a little, and then he'd sit back down.

He couldn't talk very well either.

He was slurring his words and wasn't making any sense. And I noticed his eyes weren't focused on anything either.

He was looking through us and past us.

Most of the other kids were laughing at him.

It was mildly amusing at first, but I remember feeling uncomfortable very quickly.

The thing that scared me most was how his moods changed.

He went from silly to sad to furious within seconds.

He'd be laughing one minute then crying the next.

As the laughter from the kids grew, he'd join them at first, but soon realized they were laughing *at* him and not *with* him. His laughter turned to rage, and he'd drunkenly try to stand and take a swing at the bullies.

I could smell the booze coming out of his pores too.

It was a hot day, and humid, and I remember smelling something stale and bitter, like a homeless guy I had walked past in Boston when I was younger.

I learned a few years later, after a particularly hard night of drinking in the woods, that the smell was cheap vodka.

I was hungover as hell, and a few of us went back to the woods, to see if we could find any booze we had left behind.

I found the plastic bottle I had been drinking out of, and when I unscrewed the cap and took a whiff, I almost threw up.

That's what Cliff smelled like.

The whole encounter was sad.

To be that drunk and that entirely out of control was something I never wanted to experience.

How is he going to get home? How much trouble is he going to get in? How long will he stay like that? Will he remember any of this?

I don't remember leaving Cliff in the woods that day.

I *do* remember how cruel some of the other kids were being though, poking him with a stick so he'd spin around and almost lose his balance and asking him questions just to hear his slurred speech.

I also remember asking myself why anyone would get that drunk, drunk to the point where they lost all of their faculties.

Then a few years later, when I was a freshman, I got drunk for the first time.

A friend's brother was three years older than us, but looked like he was in his mid-twenties.

He asked the four of us if we wanted a case of beer, but that it was to be drunk at his house, under his supervision, and that we'd only get six each.

Of course, we said yes.

We were in high school now.

We were practically adults.

Let's do it.

We started early on a Friday, right after school, around five.

I remember it was still light out, and it was still lovely too, so it must've been early September.

I remember looking in the fridge and seeing the case of Miller Lite staring back at me.

24 beers.

And 6 of them are mine.

God, this is so fucking cool.

I had had a few sips of my dad's beers for as far back as I can remember.

I'd be sitting on his lap at the cottage, and he'd be drinking Schlitz out of a can or Michelob out of a bottle.

I liked the fizz. I liked how cold it was too.

I wasn't allowed more than two or three sips, but I remember always wanting more.

And now here I was, with six of my own beers, right in front of me.

It was awesome.

We sat around the kitchen table playing drinking games, and by the middle of the second beer, I started feeling relaxed.

I wasn't fidgeting.

I wasn't nervously looking around, fingers plucking at my face or biting my lips.

I didn't care what others were thinking about me.

I was, finally, for once in my life, living in the moment.

And the moment was perfect.

The music was pumping (and sounded better and more alive than anything I'd ever heard).

My friends were hilarious.

Even the sun shining in the kitchen window, as it was setting over the trees, setting over my house on the next street, was more vibrant and crystalized than anything I'd ever seen.

Years later, in a college English class, we read Raymond Carver's "What We Talk About When We Talk About Love."

In essence, it's the story of four people sitting around a table, drinking the afternoon away and talking about love.

I never got a sense the story was about love

though.

"Outside in the backyard, one of the dogs began to bark. The leaves of the aspen that leaned against the window ticked against the glass. The afternoon sun was like a presence in the room, the spacious light of ease and generosity. We could have been anywhere, somewhere enchanted. We raised our glasses again and grinned at each other like children who agreed on something forbidden."

I'll never forget that paragraph.

When I read it, years after I started drinking, and already well on my way to becoming an alcoholic, that's *exactly* how I felt that day in high school.

We were children, and we were agreeing on something forbidden.

And all of it was so deliciously enchanting that I couldn't wait to do it again.

I was hooked.

By the time we were on our fourth beer, we were all pretty well lit.

We weren't black-out drunk, and it would wear off after a few hours, but it was apparent we were extremely buzzed.

But I paid for my six beers, so I was going to be damn good and sure I was going to drink them all.

We sloppily finished the rest of our booze.

I *loved* the feeling.

I felt like an adult.

I felt responsible.

I felt like I could do anything.

We stumbled out of the house and thought it'd be a brilliant idea to walk to a school dance about two miles away.

On our way, Tom bent over suddenly and unleashed all 72 oz. of his Miller Lite all over Bestick Road.

I had not (nor have I since) ever seen someone throw up with such force.

He stood up, burped, and walked on.

The rest of us laughed so hard our stomachs hurt.

If this was what was being drunk was like, then I was all for it.

When we got to the dance, Alicia and a few other girls were hanging around the side entrance to the St. Francis Assisi church, smoking cigarettes.

She was one of the prettiest girls in Braintree, and of course, I had a major crush on her, even though she was two years younger and still in junior high school.

I walked right up to her and said hi.

She not only smiled and said hi back, but she kind of jumped into my arms and hugged me.

I remember her hair tickling my face and her neck smelling of perfume.

She was so soft.

That was all it took.

On that perfect September night in 1987, I fell in love.

And I fell hard.

For the next twenty years, nothing would bring me more excitement, lust or desire than that love affair.

Nor would anything cause me more disgust, shame, and embarrassment.

In early autumn of my freshman year of high school, I fell in love with alcohol.

Chapter 4

As a freshman, thanks to the movie *Vision Quest*, I joined the Braintree High School wrestling team.

It was my first real foray into anything fitness related, and while I dreaded the practices (and was a horrible wrestler, never once winning a match), I loved what it did to my body.

I was determined to get rid of my boobs and my love handles and my double chin.

Wrestling certainly did all that.

With over two hours a day of practice (endless push-ups, sit-ups, rope climbs, and sprints, not to mention the actual wrestling) I got into fantastic shape very quickly.

But I didn't notice until a girl in my science class pulled me aside and said, "You look really good Jay."

Huh? Me? I look different?

I didn't notice a difference.

But she did, and that's all that mattered.

I was always polite if a little on the shy side, but well-liked by other kids in school. And if we were friends, I could be amusing.

But whenever I asked a girl out or had some-one do it for me (I *never* dared to be let down face to face), the reply was always the same; "Oh, he's really nice and wicked funny but, I'd rather just be friends."

So when Jen complimented me on my appearance, I felt incredible.

And other girls started to notice too.

I dated a girl for over a year during my freshman and sophomore year and fell in love.

Cathryn was her name, and two of her brothers were two of the best wrestlers the state of Massachusetts ever produced. Luckily, they were much older than me so I wasn't on the same wrestling squad.

Cathryn's dad was an alcoholic.

And every girl I would date from then until now, except for one, would also have an alcoholic father.

High school trudged along. The parties became more frequent. So did my drinking.

What had been a few beers on the occasional Friday or Saturday quickly turned into a weekly game planning event.

Who was going to get the beer? How much were we going to get? Let's get enough for Saturday night too. And maybe Sunday. It's supposed to be nice, so let's just make sure we have a few for Sunday. Just in case.

Liquor stores in Massachusetts were closed on Sundays in the late 80's so when we needed it bad enough (which was often) we'd drive the hour north to the New Hampshire state line to get more.

I never once thought twice about it.

I would've driven six hours for more booze.

The beauty of it was that I was able to buy my own booze as soon as I turned eighteen.

I was born in 1973, but Tom was able to change the 3 to look exactly like a 0 on my license. Then we laminated it so it couldn't be rubbed off.

Now that I could buy booze I had arrived.

I was the shit.

Nothing was stopping me from buying booze.

I was on my way to a liquor store ten minutes after Tom finished my ID.

We dressed me in beat-up jeans, a flannel shirt and work boots and made sure my hands were filthy, so it looked like I had just come from work. I had my dad's high school ring too, so I turned it around, so it looked like a wedding ring. I wore a baseball hat pulled down over my eyes, so I didn't have to make eye contact.

Then I was off.

I'll never forget it.

I wasn't nervous (probably because I was buzzed) and I didn't just buy a 12 pack or a case. I bought seven cases, several bottles of wine and a few 4-packs of wine coolers.

That was (and sometimes still is) my personality.

It was all or nothing.

There was nothing in moderation.

Ever.

I walked into that liquor store as an eighteen-year-old kid and then spent the next eighteen years fueling my alcoholism.

Years later, when I was a year or two sober, a bunch of my program friends and I were driving to a meeting, and we passed the same liquor store.

I told them the story as if I was bragging and I was immediately put into place by one of my buddies.

"Yeah? You bought booze there when you were younger? Cool. How'd that work out for you?"

It was like a slap in the face, but I needed it.

It put everything into perspective.

When I started regularly drinking, a 6-pack of 16 oz. beers would do the trick. But that turned into a 12-pack very quickly.

By the time I was a junior in high school it was a pint of Southern Comfort, chased by shots of Sunkist.

I felt more like an adult drinking the hard stuff.

Besides, it was easier to transport.

All I had to do was stick it in my back pocket.

When I ran out (which I usually did), I could just bum a few beers off some lightweight who couldn't or wouldn't remember if they finished theirs.

I *never* had leftover booze.

I would drink everything I had, and then I'd drink anything I could get my hands on.

It was a mental obsession that completely took over my mind. I would drink until everything was gone or I passed out.

I was the type of drunk who would become irritable or nervous when I was getting close to running out. So I always made sure I had more than enough.

Towards the end, during my last year of

drinking, I would frequent the local liquor store twice a night for two 16 oz. Coors Light and four shots (we call them "nips" in Boston) of Jose Cuervo. And that was after I had been drinking for the last three or four hours at work, just in case.

People who knew me well asked me why I just didn't buy a pint (same price as four nips but double the booze) or at least a half pint (cheaper, and one bottle instead of four).

I wasn't a drunk.

I didn't need a full pint or a half pint.

Pints were for winos who slept on park benches.

It never dawned on me that a pint was precisely what I was drinking every Friday and Saturday night in high school, almost like some dark and twisted foreshadowing of where my alcoholism would eventually take me.

Besides, the four little bottles were easier to get rid of than the half pint.

Once I did a quick shot, I could palm the bottle in my hand, and toss it into the trash without anyone knowing I had a nip in my hand.

I never littered thanks to the infamous commercial from the '70s with the crying Indian but during the last year of my drinking I did, when I walked my dogs, Elle and Grace.

It was the same exact thing every night.

I'd have two cigarettes, two Coors Light, and my four nips of Cuervo.

If there were any wine at home, I'd make sure I'd bring a "roadie" with me when I left the house.

A roadie was a drink I'd pour into a Solo cup and bring with me while I drove to the liquor store a few miles away.

The high school, where I walked my pups, was 2/10 of a mile from the house, but I was so afraid of running out of alcohol that I went completely out of my way for more.

I remembered the day I discovered a liquor store in Dorchester that was open until 11 pm on Sundays.

I was elated.

I thought it was the greatest thing in the world.

So after putting the pups into the truck and driving the 10 miles round trip to the store, I'd sit on the bleachers on the soccer field, and it'd be a party for one, or three, if you included Elle and Grace.

And I did that every fucking night for two

years.

But I'd throw the empty nip bottles over the fence behind me, vowing to come back to clean them up.

I never did.

There must've been well over a thousand by the time someone finally discovered them.

I remember another time when I was away with my then-wife.

I had been drinking all day, and when she was in the shower, I opened a bottle of wine and drank almost all of it in a few huge gulps.

But I must've got sidetracked because there was still some left right before she got out of the shower.

I remember hearing the water turn off and knew I had to finish it. Then I could get rid of the bottle under the bed, and she'd have no idea we'd ever had it in the first place.

I was chugging the last few sips when she came out of the bathroom.

She just shook her head and said, "Do you really need to finish that?"

It was the first time I had become embarrassed about my drinking, the first time I thought maybe I had a little bit of an issue.

I was just shy of my 30th birthday and would continue to drink almost daily for the next six years.

But still, regardless of the shame and embarrassment, I felt at the hands of my wife, I tilted the bottle again and finished every last drop, because that's what alcohol did to me.

I lost all thought process.

My life had one purpose and that purpose was to get drunk.

If I wasn't drunk, I was thinking about getting drunk, and if I was drunk, I was thinking about how I could get *more* drunk.

My weekend warrior days in high school soon turned into getting drunk four or five nights a week, and when I wasn't getting drunk, my friends and I would be cruising around Braintree, smoking pot.

For ten bucks we could get a case of Golden Anniversary Light and a pack of Marlboros. That was more than enough entertainment for two of us.

My friend Gene and I would sit in his car on a dead end street in a new housing development, drinking and smoking and talking about how we were going to buy an ice cream truck and drive across country, selling dope instead of ice cream.

We did that for an entire summer a few years after high school when most kids had either gone off to college, enlisted in the service, or gotten a full-time job.

Gene worked at a gas station, and I didn't have a job.

I was so good at drinking and partying that I was invited to attend summer school my senior year because I had failed math and was not allowed to graduate with my class.

But the drinking continued.

And because I wasn't wrestling anymore (or doing much of anything other than drinking and eating pizza), all the "baby fat" came back.

And then some.

A girl I was dating called me *fat,* and it devastated me.

But it certainly didn't stop me from drinking.

No way.

I was a fat, bloated mess and completely insecure about my body, but I didn't stop.

If anything, my drinking escalated.

Chapter 5

In September of 1991, a few months after I graduated, my oldest sister Kelli, was in a car accident that left her paralyzed from the waist down.

She was driving drunk, and from what she remembers, her boyfriend grabbed the steering wheel and turned it suddenly.

She went through the windshield and couldn't move.

I was at my sister Andrea's house when it happened, drinking, of course, waiting for Kelli to join us.

When she never did, I went home and passed out.

At around 5 am, my dad was banging on my bedroom door, telling me my sister had been in an accident.

No. That doesn't make sense. Dad doesn't live here. I must be dreaming.

But the banging continued and I finally stumbled out of bed and unlocked my door.

Dad was ghost white and trembling.

As we drove to University Hospital in Boston, I remember the sun coming up and that it was cold out-cold for September anyway.

Of course, I was hungover, and it wasn't lost on me that we were driving to see my sister who was just in a drunk driving accident and I was still half drunk.

Mom and Andrea were already there, and before I went in to see Kelli, Mom grabbed me by the arm and said, "Don't let her see you upset. You have to be strong."

The room was dark except for one light and the first (and only) thing I noticed was the stomach pump pumping yellowish stomach bile into a clear canister.

My nausea grew.

I edged closer to the bed and told Kelli I loved her.

She was in a head brace and was very still.

She told me she loved me and then I left the room.

I couldn't take it anymore.

The next few months were kind of a blur.

All my friends were very supportive, and we had a massive benefit for Kelli so she could raise money for a car that would be outfitted with hand controls.

The outpouring of support was incredible.

I got drunk.

I remember talking to my friend Derek right around that time, telling him I was *never* going to drive drunk, that it was stupid and reckless, and promising him that I'd never do it. He promised me he'd never do it too, or let me do it either.

That lasted two weeks.

Alcohol had such a hold on me at that point.

If I were sad, I'd drink.

Depressed? Yup.

Happy? Why not. It was okay to celebrate. I earned it.

And of course, having a sister who had just become paralyzed, who could blame me?

His sister's just been in an accident, cut him some slack.

Kelli moved in with us after being in the hospital for several months so Mom could tend to her.

My drinking got worse, and I started dabbling with cocaine.

I didn't particularly like cocaine (and utterly despised the hangover from coke), but it allowed me to stay awake for days at a time.

And when I was awake, I could drink.

One night I drank so much and had done so much cocaine, that I fell up our front steps and passed out there, after banging my head so hard on the front door that I woke Kelli up.

But nothing stopped me from drinking.

It never occurred to me that I had a problem, that my life was becoming unmanageable.

The insanity wheel just kept spinning.

I started dating Beth around that time.

Her dad was a recovering alcoholic and Beth liked to party too.

We'd drink and smoke pot almost every night, and then we'd pass out at a friends apartment.

I started experimenting with hallucinogenics, but I didn't like mushrooms or acid.

I was too paranoid, and they made me felt guilty.

Mushrooms were way too emotional, and acid lasted too long. Although with the latter, I could drink an enormous amount of alcohol, so that was a plus.

Soon after we started dating, Beth grew up (something that would take me another 17 years to do) and went back to school for exercise science. She got into fitness as well, so I decided I'd give it a whirl too.

But I had no idea what I was doing, and I was far too proud to ask anyone.

I started counting my daily fat intake instead.

At first, it was just out of curiosity.

But it became an obsession that made me deathly thin.

I started running too.

I don't know if it was because of the craze of low-fat/no-fat foods of that decade but the American public became convinced that fat was bad for us, myself included. And because I was an addict (and an addict with OCD, no less), I took my fat intake to a new (and scary) level.

I kept a notebook hidden in a drawer to track my fat intake, and within a few weeks, I had managed to get down to under 10 grams of fat a day.

The USDA recommends we eat under 50 grams a day, but 10 is too low. Fat aids in digestion, lubricate our joints, and ironically enough, it takes fat to burn fat.

Everything I bought was fat-free; fat-free pasta sauce, fat-free cream cheese, fat-free hot dogs.

I honestly thought because the label said "Fat-Free," that it was healthy.

Not only was I depriving my body of healthy fats, but I was starving myself.

Breakfast would consist of a bagel or sometimes a fat-free blueberry muffin from Dunkin' Donuts. Lunch would be a tuna sandwich with fat-free mayonnaise and dinner would either be pasta or fat-free hot dogs with fat-free baked beans.

That was my Monday-Wednesday.

On Thursday I'd drive the 35 minutes back to Braintree (I was living in Jamaica Plain at the time) to hang at our local watering hole.

And then I'd gorge.

I'd get fishcakes with mac n cheese and a basket of fries.

And of course, I'd wash it all down with at least a dozen draft beers.

But I remember salivating as soon as I walked into the bar.

My body was craving food.

I was starving myself during the week and thought it was perfectly natural.

I'm getting thinner. My runs are getting longer. I must be doing something right.

One night, Gene and I drove to Braintree, and on the way home, he decided to see how fast his car could go.

I have no idea why I put my seatbelt on (I never wore it back then-it was uncool), but I did.

Something told me to.

Two minutes after getting on the highway (and driving more than 100 mph) Gene lost control of the car.

We spun around two and a half times and slammed into the Jersey barrier.

I was stuck.

My door wouldn't open.

Gene scrambled out of his seat, said he was sorry, and ran across the other three lanes of the highway and disappeared into a marsh.

I was finally able to crawl out his side and then ran to Beth's house.

Her door was unlocked, so I snuck up to her bedroom, told her what happened, then passed out in her basement.

She gave me a ride to work the next day, and I was so hungover that a friend gave me a Percocet.

I don't remember it doing anything, but my hangover went away.

Gene called to apologize for taking off, and I just laughed it off.

I never once thought it was a big deal, even though Gene was practically in tears when he called, telling me he was sorry over and over again, that he could've killed me.

Friday nights Beth and I would eat a light dinner, and we'd be sensible all day Saturday. Sunday we splurged a bit on a late lunch, and then I'd have to go back to Jamaica Plain to clean the spotless house I had left 48 hours before.

That was a must.

Beth would sit in my room, and study, and I'd clean the entire house.

Then the entire cycle would start over again the next day.

I lost 30 lb. in a little over 6 months and had become too skinny.

Between the lack of fat and running 3 miles a day, I was emaciated.

Not only had I lost a lot of fat but I lost a ton of muscle too.

I had set out to lose weight though, and that's what I did, so I was happy for the most part.

I figured that because I wasn't drinking Monday-Wednesday and not on Sundays either, I was controlling it.

I could manage it.

I had no idea the void was now being filled with my new fitness/fat counting hobby.

I still drank but not as much.

I'm getting in shape. All is perfect in the world.

Someone told me years later, that when people have to think about controlling something, no matter what it is, it's because it's out of control.

That makes sense now.

It didn't then.

In April of 1996, I was hired by the phone company, and everything fell into place.

I had a great job.

I had a great girl I was going to marry and have kids with. We'd buy a house and maybe even a summer house someday, just like my dad.

But booze crept back into my life and became more important than my health.

It was more important than anything, including the girl I was dating, the girl I had every intention of marrying.

Sometimes life doesn't work out the way we plan.

Or at all, when alcohol calls the shots.

Chapter 6

After I broke up with Beth, I went on a drinking rampage that lasted another ten years.

Alcoholism is a progressive disease and mine had progressed to the point of utter disgust.

The choices I was making, the things I was doing, and the people I was hurting were never an issue for me.

I never gave it a second thought because I didn't care.

I wanted what I wanted, and I wanted it now, and I was going to do anything to get it.

And all I wanted to do was drink.

And drink I did.

Constantly.

The day I broke up with Beth, I walked into her house after being out all night with Tom, sat on her bed, told her I loved her but wasn't in love with her, and said I wanted to break up.

Then I told her parents and walked out of her life.

I had been living with Beth and her parents for over a year after abruptly moving out of Jamaica Plain because I couldn't stand my roommates.

Yeah...and that had nothing to do with you being an anal-retentive control freak with a touch of passive-aggressiveness?

Nope. It was all their *fault.*

I had recently moved into an apartment.

In the process of renting the apartment, I met the landlord's daughter (she was in charge of screening the applicants) and decided I didn't want to be with Beth anymore and that this new girl, Farrah, would be a better choice.

So after being with Beth for five years, I broke up with her suddenly and spent the same night with Farrah.

I now know that it was just a ruse to get out of a relationship.

I didn't dare admit my faults in the relationship or my character defects and certainly wasn't going to take any of the blame myself. So I just removed myself from the equation, without any thought or concern for the girl who was by my side for the last half-decade.

That would become a habit for me.

If I didn't like you or if you didn't agree with me and my views of the world, I'd walk out of your life.

I did it with girls, friends, and even walked out of my mother's life for four years because of my stubbornness.

Farrah didn't last long.

She was much older than me and had a kid.

I was *way* too selfish to consider being a part-time dad.

I didn't date much for the next year or so but it indeed wasn't for lack of trying.

Now, instead of drinking at friend's houses and in the woods, as I did in high school, I was old enough to drink legally.

I was living alone.

I was single.

I was making good money with the phone company.

Weekends were one long, blurry mess and I ended up spending much more than I ever made, even though we were usually comped every Friday night at our watering hole in Boston. I didn't know the guys who would charge five of us $19 for a full night of drinking, and I didn't care.

All I cared about was drinking until I blacked out.

The funny thing is because I'd drink alone before I'd go out, I'd be too drunk ever to initiate a conversation with a girl.

I'd be "That Guy" in the corner, grinning stupidly and not remembering a thing, nor talking to anyone.

My friend Stevie would wander over from time to time, and ask if I was okay.

"I'm good," I'd reply, which, as both of us knew very well, meant I was out of my fucking mind, but I wasn't going to do anything stupid or rash.

It was those few times when I'd say I was a mess or drunk that Stevie knew enough to take me home or, on more than one occasion, help me into the back of my Ford F-100 (complete with cap and bed) so I could pass out.

He once found me laying on my back, passed out, snoring loudly, and I had an open Rolling Rock bottle still gripped in my hand.

I had snuck it out of the bar, which was nothing new.

But the sick part was that I couldn't let go of the fucking bottle, even when I was passed out.

It was the world's most addictive and insane security blanket.

During the few days when I didn't drink, mostly because I just needed a break and my body was exhausted, I was incredibly lonely.

I remember hooking up with a girl I had gone to high school with and for the next week I called her and begged her to come over so incessantly that she finally told me to get a grip and to leave her alone entirely.

I had become a desperate, needy person and I was sick over it.

But I kept right on drinking.

———————————

I drank because I was trying to fill a void, a void that continued to grow the more I drank, so it became a vicious circle, and I could never get enough.

I felt lost, alone, desolate, scared, and completely unsure of myself.

Drinking didn't solve any of those problems, but it pushed the emotions far enough down to where I didn't have to think about them or think about anything in fact.

I was what some people call a *functioning*

alcoholic.

But I like what a friend of mine says better-I was just a drunk with a job.

I worked for the phone company for almost fifteen years before I was forced into retirement (in essence being fired for the second time from a union job because of my drinking).

Right from the first day, I hated it.

I hated the mentality of union workers (do as little work as possible for fantastic pay and benefits and then complain about it). I hated the job itself (I just wasn't passionate about giving people dial tone), and I hated the union vs. management mentality.

But it was a good job (or career, all of my friends would say) so I stuck with it.

I made sure I did as little work as possible and went to even greater lengths to do it with an attitude.

The one good thing about working there was that there were a bunch of other guys who liked to drink as much as I did.

It started with a few of us going out on Fridays after work but that soon progressed into Thursdays too.

By the time I was transferred from Roslindale

to South Boston about five years in, my shift had changed to the noon to eight crew, and my drinking took on a whole new level.

I was drinking every night on the job.

Boston is predominantly a blue-collar, hard-working city and there is a bar on almost every corner.

It's a small city area-wise, in comparison to New York, Los Angeles, and Chicago, but there is no shortage of bars.

One day I wrote down all the bars in Boston proper, which included the Fenway Park area, The South End (not to be confused with South Boston, which I also wrote down), Back Bay, Beacon Hill, The West End (a neighborhood most suburbanites don't even know about), The North End, downtown, and Charlestown.

There were over 100 bars.

I had been to all of them except for two in Southie, and the only reason I didn't go into those two was that people from Southie told me if an outsider went into them, they may not come out.

And I had been to all of them while I was working.

That's the kind of freedom I had with my job.

I was all over the city, doing as little work as possible, and a few hours before my shift ended, I'd park my truck close to where it was supposed to be and walk to the closest bar.

A shot of Cuervo and an Amstel Light was always how I started, to get things going.

Sometimes I'd meet up with a few guys from work, but most times I'd drink alone. Sometimes I'd get dinner and sometimes I wouldn't.

But I always managed to get buzzed enough to feel some semblance of normalcy.

Then, on the way back to the garage, I'd stop at a liquor store on West Broadway in Southie and get four more shots of Cuervo and two cans of Coors Light.

I went there because they never judged me.

They never looked at me funny, even when they saw me sway a little, climbing from my work truck and sauntering towards them. It got to the point where as soon as they saw me, they'd have my small brown bag already wrung up and waiting on the counter.

That'd be enough to last me the 8-mile commute to Milton, and if I was lucky enough (and could control myself), it was enough to last me until I went to walk the pups at the high school.

I'd hit another liquor store and do the same thing all over again-4 shots and 2 16 oz. Coors Lights.

Just shy of fourteen drinks in less than three hours, not including whatever I drank when I was on the clock.

But I didn't have a drinking problem.

No way.

I got up and went to work. I paid my bills. I was a nice enough guy.

I deserved to have a few drinks after (and maybe sometimes during) work.

And the entire time I never once thought I had an issue.

Nor did anyone else.

So I kept going.

Chapter 7

I was never impressed with a person's war stories.

I always felt like they were trying to glorify what they did-the insane amount of booze they drank or the copious amounts of drugs they snorted, shot, or swallowed.

"I spilled more beer than you ever drank," was one of the most annoying sayings I've heard people say from the podium.

Yeah. I get it.

You drank a lot. Didn't we all?

Isn't that why we're all crammed in this dank church basement, trying to get through just one more day of being sober?

I always felt there was a difference between glorifying what we did when we were active versus sharing some of our experience when we were out there.

My story is mild compared to some as far as jails, institutions or death are concerned, but I earned my seat in recovery.

Besides, it's not about comparison.

It's about being able to relate to other

alcoholics, to see the similarities we had, regardless of age, sex or social class.

In all my years of drinking, I only got in trouble once.

I was visiting a friend at Worcester State College, and decided it'd be a brilliant idea to take a hit of acid *after* drinking a half fifth of Southern Comfort.

It wasn't.

I finished the rest of the fifth and the rest of the night was (and still is) a mixed up jumble of images.

I vaguely remember being screamed at because I tried to pass out on the kitchen floor, running through the woods, being questioned by campus security, challenging someone to a fight, waking up covered in mud in clothes that weren't mine, and limping around campus because I had lost one shoe.

When security caught up with me for the second time, the first question they asked was, "Where's your other shoe?"

"I got jumped by four kids, and they only wanted the left one," I replied.

They arrested me immediately and hogtied me.

I was placed on my belly, and my wrists were handcuffed to my ankles.

And that's how I spent the night in jail.

When I tried to find my way back to the college the next morning, a traffic cop laughed out loud and shook his head when he saw me hobbling his way, asking for directions.

I had to return to the Worcester court system a few months later and received a "Persona Non Grata" letter from Worcester State College.

I was never allowed back.

I was also instructed to attend my first 12 step meeting that afternoon and to report back to the judge immediately upon completion.

I sat in the back, eating donuts and laughing every time someone announced their name and said they were an alcoholic.

What a bunch of fucking losers.

I was never arrested again.

I never got into any fights (although I was jumped once) and I never got a DUI, although I was stopped drunk a half dozen times.

I was pulled over twice in my hometown, and both times, the cop asked what was in the Solo cup.

"Water," I replied both times. There was also Ketel One vodka in it too, but he didn't need to know that.

After sniffing it and handing it back to me, he told me to get where I was going and to stay there.

I never became nasty or belligerent.

If anything, I was more relaxed and happy when I was drunk.

That's why I kept drinking.

I was miserable sober.

I had too much junk bouncing around in my head, too many insecurities, too much self-doubt, and self-hatred. I was way too concerned about what others thought (although would never admit it) and was so utterly afraid of everything.

But I knew alcohol could quell those issues.

At least temporarily.

Or in my case, permanently, if I could get away with drinking every day.

Alcoholism is a mental disease.

The booze leaves our bodies in 72 hours.

It's the mental part of alcoholism that's so hard to overcome.

The obsession to have just one more drink, whether we've had none or nine, is always there when we're actively drinking.

Even when we stop for a brief period, the itch will eventually make its way back unless we get help.

I never had any problem stopping. That was easy for me.

But I couldn't stay stopped.

I was a binge drinker to the extreme.

Not once did I find it odd, sick or dangerous to wake up after a night of drinking and drink again.

Immediately.

And then I'd drink for the rest of the day, especially during weekends and vacations, and repeat that process until I had to go back to reality.

The first time I went to Las Vegas I had the second anxiety attack of my life.

I woke up with one of the worst hangovers I've ever had and made the mistake of taking two Excedrin on an empty stomach.

I wasn't a caffeine drinker so as soon as the Excedrin made its way into my bloodstream, I was wired beyond belief.

I thought the world was coming to an end and knew only one thing would make me feel better. I had to meet some of my wife's friends for brunch, and when they saw me, they immediately knew that something was off.

So did Bella, my wife.

I excused myself to go to the bathroom, and Bella pulled me aside and asked if I was okay.

"No," I said, "I'm having an anxiety attack and need a shot of tequila."

"Now?" she said "it's ten o'clock in the morning."

"Yes. Now."

As soon as I drank it, I felt better. Then I had several beers with brunch.

I was drunk again by noon.

The rest of the trip was a blur.

Some people grimace or gag when I say I loved the taste of alcohol, especially tequila. But I did.

I loved it all.

I loved beer, wine, vodka, gin, rum, tequila, whiskey, and scotch.

Not only did I love the taste, but I loved everything about it.

I loved the sexiness of it.

I loved sitting at a bar, listening to the ice clink in the glass as the bartender poured.

I loved the anticipation, the smell, the taste,

and of course, the feeling.

I felt adult, distinguished, mature.

It never once occurred to me that I was just your average garden variety drunk.

I thought because I liked so many different types, and was just as comfortable sipping wine at The Four Seasons as I was guzzling beer at Fenway Park, that I was cultured.

I'm worldly. I'm a man of the world. I can roll with the best of them.

I was fucking pathetic, is what I was.

I never thought it was strange to drink alone either.

I thought it was the most natural thing in the world.

When I lived alone, I had a ritual that involved chilling two Rolling Rocks and a nip of Cuervo in my freezer when I showered.

The radio would be blasting, my clothes would be laid out (I wasn't drunk yet, so the OCD was in full force), and I'd crack the first beer before I got dressed.

I'd have four or five drinks before I went out for the night.

It was normal for me, and I can't remember a

time when I *didn't* drink before going out.

There was a time in my late 20's where I went to over a dozen weddings.

I wasn't even close to remotely sober by the time I made it to the ceremony.

By the time the reception started, I was three or four drinks away from a blackout.

The sad thing is, I always drove.

I didn't like taxi's and would never take public transportation.

I couldn't be in control if someone else were driving.

And the even sadder thing (and have friends who can attest to this) is that I had a mini bar in the console of my Dodge Ram, complete with soda water, lemons, a cutting board, and knife.

I would always bring an extra cup of ice too.

Me, my Solo cup, and my mini-bar and I'd be all set.

I bought Grey Goose or Ketel One because it was high end.

I wasn't discriminating against cheaply made vodka.

I was told that good quality vodka is hard to smell, especially when mixed with lemon, so I bought high-end vodka.

I've heard people talk about how they never had any fun when they were drinking, that they did it to fit in or to get outside of themselves.

But I had a blast in the beginning.

I was young, had a pocket full of money, and always had at least two or three friends willing to go off the deep end with me.

There was such a sense of freedom to being an adult, to being able to do what I wanted, when I wanted, and to not have to answer to anyone or reign myself in.

I've seen Ireland, the majority of the Pacific Coast Highway, Bermuda, a ton of Florida, and almost all of New England.

I've been to dozens of concerts, cocktail parties, company outings, and conventions in Las Vegas and New York City.

And I was drunk for all of it.

One time, days after getting approved for a $10,000 credit card, Tom and I decided to fly to an exotic place, just for the hell of it.

I had recently been suspended from the phone company but never thought twice about racking up debt.

But because Tom was afraid to fly we drove to South Station in Boston, parked his Jeep, and told the ticket lady to give us a train ticket to anywhere she wanted.

After a ten minute debate (and her not believing us) she gave us a one-way ticket to Baltimore (the furthest destination from Boston).

By the time we reached New York, Tom was drunk enough to fly, but because both New York airports were fogged in, we kept going.

I was blacked out when we finally reached Baltimore, and according to the train conductor, Tom and I cleaned out the bar.

We had the same conductor on the return trip and, according to him, we cleaned the bar out then too.

I'm not sure I believed him though.

I'm sure he heard us say we had to drive when we got back to Boston, so he probably shut us off.

Tom and I would purposely try to get shut off at places that were strict about the liquor laws in Massachusetts.

I've been shut off at every Chili's I've ever visited.

I wore that badge of "honor" like it was a

Purple Heart, thinking I was cool and giving me something to brag about to my friends.

Most of them just shook their head in disgust.

When we got to Baltimore, we checked into a hotel, passed out, then got up the next day and took the train back to Boston.

By the time we reached home, Tom was again drunk enough to fly, but somehow I talked him out of going on another trip.

The Jeep was locked in a parking lot (I don't remember parking it there) so Tom drove it through the fence without a second thought.

That was just a typical day for me when I was drinking.

I thought it was funny.

A few of my close friends were starting to become concerned.

But I didn't listen.

Tell me to do something, and I'll do the exact opposite. Tell me *not* to do something, and I'll do it anyway-several times.

I woke up in a circus tent once (don't ask because I don't remember anything after downing three shots of tequila and a few beers on an empty stomach at a bar owned by Aerosmith in Del Ray Beach).

I woke up half in, half out of a rental car in a Ft. Lauderdale beach parking lot.

I've lost many sunglasses, jackets, wallets, and a snowboard because I was drunk.

On more than one occasion I lost my truck, which was probably a good thing, because I would've driven it if I could've found it.

I bought a boa constrictor once because I thought it'd be a good idea to own a snake, shit myself right before I was supposed to show up for work, and lost an entire day over one Labor Day weekend in the late '90s in a blackout.

I woke up Monday morning excited that we still had another day and a half of drinking.

When my friends told me it was Monday, and not Sunday, I didn't believe them.

It took the hotel desk lady and two local news stations to convince me otherwise.

Another time at the lake I drank a twelve pack in under two hours in the blazing sun.

A few hours later I woke up in the boat, drifting aimlessly.

During the few months that I was dabbling with cocaine, I came out of a blackout roaming around the hallways of a New York City hotel, in nothing but a bathrobe and jeans. I had so much energy that I paced the halls for over four hours. I tried to drink enough to calm down or pass out, but it never happened.

Tom and I went to New York to see U2 a few years later, and after spending the following day in the city with our friend (and having at least 15 drinks), we got high, and started the four-hour drive back to Boston.

Tom got tired when he was coming down from being high, so he told me to take over. He jumped in the back seat as I scrambled over to the driver's seat.

It was windy and rainy, and we were going over 60 mph when he did it.

I remember giggling so hard for the next half hour that my stomach hurt.

I thought it was funny.

I blacked out at a bar in Florida, and woke up in a strange man's car.

He was rubbing my leg and trying to unzip my pants.

I jumped out of the car and ran to a gas station then blacked out again. I came out of the blackout a second time on the balcony of the hotel I was staying at because I had smashed the window to get into the room.

The pain snapped me back to reality.

My keys and wallet were in my backpack in the man's car, I think. I know I had it with me when I walked into the bar a few hours before.

I went to a concert in Allston and drank so many tequila shots before the show that I was kicked out after the second song. I came out of the blackout when two college kids were picking me up off the floor of their building entryway. They threw me in the bushes where I passed out again.

I woke up the next day with cuts and bruises all over my arms and legs. I must've taken a cab home because I had my keys but not my truck.

Tom drove me back to Allston, and I promised myself I wasn't going to drink that day.

After we drove around for two hours trying to find my truck, I asked him if he wanted to get drunk.

It was early afternoon on a Monday. He thought about it for two seconds and said yes.

I was blacked out again by the time it got dark that night.

I was given a Percocet in the middle of a party, but complained it didn't work, so was given an other one.

I had to be carried home.

My dad said he had never seen me so drunk.

I guess pills and booze don't mix.

Besides, pills are for loser junkies, I thought, *and I'm not an addict.*

I broke my hand in Las Vegas, after punching the hotel room mirror.

I had been taking a fat burner, and it clearly said not to mix it with alcohol.

It made me insanely angry, and earlier that night I met a co-worker of Bella's.

He was rude to me while ogling her, but I didn't take it out on him. I took it out on Bella, and the mirror in our room.

I drank for the rest of the night (enough to pass out) then woke up the next morning with a swollen hand and one of the worst hangovers of my life.

The shot they gave me to readjust my hand was the single most painful thing I've ever experienced. I bucked off the examining table.

Tom and I went to a party once, and a friend opened his trunk and showed us a duffle bag full of mushrooms.

We both grabbed a handful and ate them.

Within twenty minutes we were both out of our minds.

A tropical storm hit the area suddenly, and one of the girls who was doing mushrooms had a seizure. As soon as the ambulance came, and the lights were flashing everywhere, Tom and I both freaked.

It was like that scene from *Apocalypse Now,* when the guns and fireworks are going off everywhere, and no one can make sense of what's going on.

We ran to his Jeep, which was parked by the ocean, and for some reason I climbed underneath it, even though it was pouring rain and windy.

I remember feeling extremely hot but remember that my back was cool because it was wet.

I also remember Tom pointing to the sky and screaming that the dragons were going to get us. I looked and did see a dragon form in one of the lightning blasts.

I must've passed out at that point, but I do remember dreaming (or I may have been awake and hallucinating) that I was on my deathbed, and that my entire family was around me. I couldn't talk but could hear them.

I don't remember what they were saying but I remember that I flatlined.

Every once in a while I still have flashbacks of that deathbed scene.

Sometimes I think I'm still on the deathbed (and have been for years), and my family is trying to decide if they should unhook me from life support.

Sometimes I think it was just a huge sign, that I was so close to the edge, and that if I didn't stop I *would* die.

I have never been that out of my mind in my life (not even close), and it scared me.

I came to when I heard Tom talking to one of my co-workers.

When he asked Tom where I was, Tom calmly said, "He's under the Jeep."

Of course, my co-worker didn't believe him (who would?).

He laughed and drove away.

Then I remember sitting up in the back of the Jeep, driving down the highway, and Tom started throwing up all over the steering wheel and windshield.

I started crying (mushrooms are *that* emotional), and told him that I loved him, and didn't want him to die and that he should pull over so I could drive.

He barked that he was fine in between hurling.

I passed out again.

We laughed about it the next day.

Then we got drunk.

My intent at the beginning of all of these nights was to go out, relax, be sociable, and have a good time.

It failed every time.

I have no idea why I couldn't control it. But I couldn't.

The funny thing was that I knew when I was buzzed. I knew when I was drunk. And I knew when I was one or two drinks away from a blackout.

But I just kept going.

A reasonable person would probably stop after being buzzed.

Maybe they'd stay out a little later if they knew they could get home safely, didn't have much going on the next day or just wanted to let loose a bit.

But that was never a choice in my mind.

I was going to drink until I blacked out.

It was never my intent before I drank. But once I took the first sip, all bets were off.

I was gone.

The only time I succeeded in stopping after a few drinks was the night before a sprint triathlon.

I had been training for six weeks and knew if I got drunk I'd never get up in time for the race.

But the restlessness and irritability set in, and before I knew it, I was walking out of a liquor store with a six-pack of 16 oz. Coors Light.

I have this fucking drinking thing under control. Who says I don't? I only got a six pack. Granted, it's eight beers, because they're 16 oz. But at least I didn't get a twelve-pack. And I didn't get any nips either. So there's that.

I have this thing under control.

I remember getting antsy as I opened the last one, but I had timed it so I couldn't go back out and get more.

Besides, I'm a triathlete now. I need my rest so I can do well tomorrow.

I thought my actions were normal that night.

I've heard that it's not the eighth or ninth drink that takes the man, but that it's the first one.

I didn't understand that for years.

But I do now.

The mental obsession to have another one never diminishes.

It grows as the night goes on.

I could never have just one. Or two.

I remember when I was going through a particularly bad time.

I was living in Somerville, just north of Boston, and I was sitting in a bar talking to a good friend.

I was telling him I thought I drank too much, and he completely agreed. He was telling me about how he was going to contact my family (I was living with him at the time), because he was concerned I was out of control.

He put his beer down suddenly and said, "Let's go. Let's just stop now. We don't need to finish these."

I was floored.

I looked at him like he was insane.

I told him no and ordered another one.

He shook his head. Then he got up and left.

I have no idea how I got home.

I have *never* left a drink half finished.

And back when smoking was allowed in bars,

I'd cringe when people would extinguish cigarette butts in half a glass of booze.

What a total waste of a drink!

Who in the world would think it's a travesty of justice when even a sip of alcohol is used as an ashtray?

An alcoholic would.

I would.

My drunken escapades continued.

I broke into a friend's cabana to steal booze but could only find Kahlua.

I drank it straight because I didn't have anything to mix it with, then spent the night throwing up in my basement sink.

I blamed it on a friend when my mom asked about it the next day.

I went to a softball party, smoked two joints, and drank so many beers so fast that I vaguely remember being laughed at on the train ride home and my mom screaming at me that I had a problem.

I was half passed out on my bed, and it wasn't even dark outside when she found me.

I dove into shallow water drunk twice, the first time perforating my bowel (still have the scar), and the second time landing on my head.

Luckily, the bottom of the lake was so sandy it almost acted like a cushion. And even though I was ridiculously drunk at the time, when I reached the surface of the water, I knew that had been a close one.

Of course, I kept right on drinking.

I knocked a kids teeth out, and got sued for it when I was drinking.

One night, after the bar closed, a gentleman informed me that he wanted to smash a ball peen hammer off my forehead until I was dead.

I put my arm around him and told him to think about rainbows and Smurfs instead.

If we weren't in a crowd or if I was just a tiny bit drunker, he may very well have done just that.

I drank cooking wine when I ran out of both regular booze, and reasons to run to the store because I knew it had at least a little alcohol in it.

I showed up at a funeral with two nips of Jose Cuervo in my suit jacket.

People were already gathered at the grave, but I *needed* that booze so I leaned over into the passenger seat and drank them both, one right after the other.

I put the empty nips in my overcoat pocket

and played with them as I stood at the grave.

It gave me comfort and made me feel safe.

But no, I didn't have a drinking problem.

Not at all.

Part III: The Hangover

"Sounds fine to me," I said. "Eat or not eat. Or keep drinking. I could head right on out into the sunset."

"I could eat something myself," Laura said. "I don't think I've ever been so hungry in my life. Is there something to nibble on?"

"I'll put out some cheese and crackers," Terri said.

But Terri just sat there. She did not get up to get anything.

Mel turned his glass over. He spilled it out on the table.

"Gin's gone," Mel said.

Terri said, "Now what?"

I could hear my heart beating. I could hear everyone's heart. I could hear the human noise we sat there making, not one of us moving, not even when the room went dark."

~Raymond Carver

Chapter 8

I met Bella on April 27th, 1998.

She had three kids and lived in a very nice house in Milton, the next town over from Braintree.

I had been sent to her house to test her phone line, and when I was done, I was sitting in my work truck, doing paperwork.

"Are you going to fix my phone?" she said, scaring the hell out of me.

I was instantly attracted to her, but it was a Friday, and Friday's were party time, so I went about my weekend, getting annihilated for the next 48 hours.

But when Monday came around, I had the brilliant idea to go back to her house and ask her if she had found one of my tools that I may have accidentally left there.

That type of behavior, the kind where I never stop to think that what I was doing was irresponsible, dangerous or just plain stupid, was totally the norm.

Alcoholics are self-centered and completely selfish by nature.

But something happens to me when I'm hungover.

It's almost like I have a third personality, the first being Sober Jay and the second Drunk Jay.

When I'm hungover, I have no filter, no reservations, no tact.

I want what I want, and I want it now, and I'm going to ask for it, no matter what it is. There is no forethought, nor any decision making. I go for it.

So I drove back to Bella's house because she was attractive and I was lonely.

Cell phones weren't readily available yet, so I left her my beeper number, never expecting her to call, but taking the chance anyway.

She did.

And that began our 13-year relationship.

The fact that she had three babies never occurred to me. Nor did the fact that I very easily could've lost my job because of my actions.

Even writing this sentence makes me sick.

Instant gratification was something I thought I deserved.

I think that's why drinking worked so well for me at the beginning.

The way that first drink felt as it coursed through my veins and warmed me up was instantaneous.

Even on the days when I was so hungover, I could barely function, by the third drink, I'd at least be feeling normal again.

I'd shoot the first two fast, get past the nausea, and try to stomach the third one, usually a beer.

By the time it was finished, I'd be okay.

I fell hard for Bella, and I fell fast.

She rented a house, and within two years I was part of the family.

I was a 28-year-old immature kid, with a severe drinking problem, trying to be a stepdad to three little kids, who I adored, but had no idea how to raise.

I couldn't even take care of myself, never mind three babies.

Somewhere towards the beginning, after a particularly raucous weekend, Bella said as much to me.

"I have three kids. I don't want another one," she told me.

It sunk in a little.

But it certainly didn't stop me or slow me down.

Bella got a great job, and because we were both making good money, I did the responsible thing, and I partied like a rock star.

We ate out at least three times a week, traveled extensively because of her work, and bought cars, computers, and clothes like we were millionaires.

And while eating out a few times a week may not seem like an extravagant expense, I've done the math.

Between the drinks and because the types of places we ate at were usually high end (my friend Bob used to call me the "Jet-set Phone Man") our average bill was well over $100. Multiply that by three nights a week, and we were spending over $1200 a month on dinner alone.

That was half of our mortgage.

But I never thought twice about it because we had the money.

We had fun when we were drinking, and saw some amazing places, but because of the way we met and because alcohol fueled the fire, there was never any basis for a solid foundation. Our relationship didn't stand a chance because of alcoholism.

There were trust issues from the beginning.

I was extremely insecure, and Bella is extremely attractive, and the attention she received when we went out used to drive me nuts, even though she always assured me that I was the one she wanted to be with.

My OCD had blown out of control too because I felt so lost.

Why is she with someone like me? What does she see in me? Is she going to leave me for some guy who treats her better? Someone with more money?

It was an awful way to live, to be that insecure, and no matter what Bella said or did, I couldn't overcome it.

Someone once told me that people suffer from OCD, and the need to control everything on the outside, because they are so fucked up on the inside.

That's *exactly* how I felt.

I was a drunk, but I was a neat and organized drunk, and trying to live with four other people was next to impossible for me.

The amount of time I spent cleaning up and vacuuming paled in comparison to the time I should've spent being present in their lives.

And I knew that.

Bella pointed it out a few times, but instead of taking a step back and listening, I'd get defensive and try to argue that a clean house was more important than playing with the kids.

That went on for a decade.

The definition of insanity is doing the same thing over and over again and expecting different results.

I was insane.

We were in South Beach once, and although I hadn't had a drink in over nine months, I had the brilliant idea of doing a shot of Patron.

Why not? We're on vacation. I'll stop again when we get home.

We ordered the shot, and I'll never forget how I felt it coursing through my veins, from the tip of my tongue all the way to my toes.

Ahhhh.

I'm home.

This is what I'm supposed to be doing. This is it. This is what I love, and this is what I'm going to do.

The rest of the trip was a booze-filled blur and although we did have fun (we always had fun when we traveled), it was going back to reality that kept causing problems.

We couldn't communicate.

I'd be too quick to lose my temper, and be

cause of that, she'd suppress a lot of what she was feeling and, in essence, sweep everything under the rug.

The lack of communication between us was staggering.

We'd have periods when things would be great.

I'd stop drinking, get involved in a fitness regimen and we'd be well on our way to getting back to living the American dream.

Bella ran fitness clubs in her 20's and is a certified yoga instructor, so she was always into fitness.

I joined the same gym she belonged to, even though I thought I was too good for gyms.

I'll figure this whole fitness thing out on my own.

I was a fan of bodyweight exercises because they could be performed anywhere.

But more importantly, they could be performed alone.

I was so concerned about what other people thought and so afraid that people would be able to see through my facade, that I acted like a stuck-up, arrogant tool.

Deep down I knew I wasn't too good for

gyms.

I was insecure and horrified that I'd walk into a gym and have no idea what I was doing. It was that feeling that I was "less than," the sense that people were looking at me and judging me.

But I joined and fumbled my way through workouts that I either found online or read in fitness magazines.

I didn't particularly enjoy working out but soon realized that I could sweat my hangovers out.

How I'd walk into a gym and exercise hungover is something I'll never understand, but I did.

I didn't get in shape, because of all the alcohol I was drinking.

———————————————

I was never an angry drunk.

If anything, I was friendlier, and goofier when I was drinking.

When I was drinking, my OCD all but disappeared. I didn't mind the mess and the chaos. I was off in Drunkland somewhere.

It was when I *wasn't* drinking that I was almost unbearable.

I had a short fuse.

I was irritable and snapped at the kids a lot, especially Liz. Liz had only two speeds-full throttle or asleep, so that could be exhausting at times.

I remember when she was seven years old and we were turning onto our street.

Before I even took the turn, she was opening the door. Of course, she almost fell out. I had to grab her and pull her back in.

Then I yelled at her.

She started crying.

I never screamed at the kids but she scared the hell out of me.

And I felt horrible for yelling at her, watching her little chin quiver, and her huge blue eyes well up.

She didn't realize she had almost fallen out of a moving car. That's what type of kid she was. She was always living, thinking, and moving two steps in the future. But I never considered that.

Everything was always all about me.

When I was irritable, I could be a dick.

When things weren't going my way, I could be a dick. When there were too many people in the house, and all my cleaning duties were interrupted, I could be a dick.

Everything had to be in my control.

I had to be the director of everything that was going on around me. And if things weren't going the way I wanted them to, I'd be unbearable.

Weekend mornings were especially tough.

I'd be hungover, and the house would be loud and busy, and we'd usually have at least three (and sometimes as many as nine) other kids in the house.

I couldn't relax. I couldn't let things go. I couldn't sit still.

And the kids could sense that.

Both Bella and the kids always felt like they were walking on eggshells.

I was only normal after a few drinks, but in the beginning, I didn't drink during the day.

The only time I drank during the day was when Bella and I were away. I knew enough (and had enough control) to not drink during the day when the kids were around.

So I'd grit my teeth and somehow get through it.

But as my alcoholism progressed, I drank more and more, no matter who was around. And I was very good at hiding it.

There were several instances with the kids and my drinking that scared the hell out of me. I knew I was out of control but didn't know how to stop.

And even if I did, I didn't want to.

I couldn't possibly fathom going through life without drinking.

One day, I was with Bella's youngest, Joey, and two of his buddies.

We were driving somewhere close, but I needed booze, so I stopped and grabbed a couple of nips of Cuervo and hid them in my pocket.

I was already buzzed because I never would've done this sober (at least that's what I tell myself).

All four of us were in my Dodge Ram, so we were all in front, on the bench seat.

The boys were messing around, and I was able to get one of the nips out of my pocket.

When they weren't looking, I drank it.

I made sure it was wrapped entirely in my hand, but it didn't matter.

Jose Cuervo has a very distinct, powerful, leathery smell.

Joey stopped messing around for a minute, and asked what that smell was.

I made up a lie.

He knew I was lying. I could tell by the look in his eye. But I didn't care.

The booze was in my blood, and it was doing its job, and I was satisfied, for now.

But I promised myself I'd never do that again.

Of course, it wasn't because I thought I was irresponsible.

It was because I didn't want to get caught. If I got caught maybe someone would be on to my little drinking problem.

And I was nowhere near ready to stop.

I became more and more irresponsible, putting myself and the lives of my family in danger.

A few years later I was at the lake with my family.

Joey, my nephews and niece, and Elle and Grace were all at Weirs Beach, a cheesy tourist spot packed with arcades, mini-golf and of course, bars.

Brian, my brother, was with us too.

We had been drinking for the better part of the afternoon, although at this point my family thought I was sober.

I had recently finished my second stint in detox, but was controlling my drinking, so I was doing fine, in my mind.

I had a half gallon of vodka stashed under the seat of my truck, and every half hour, I'd wander outside, and over to my truck to add a little to my soda water and lemon.

I've never been able to explain it and don't understand it, but as I said earlier, people could barely tell when I was drunk.

I was normal, other than smiling a little more, and acting a bit sillier.

Brian was the same way.

But Brian knew when I was drinking.

He and I are only 14 months apart ("one year, two months, five days, and seven hours" we'd tell people), and he never questioned anything I did, whether it was good, bad, insane, or dangerous.

And I loved him for it.

He never judged, never asked questions, never shook his head in disgust, and was always willing to kill anyone who even looked at me wrong.

I'm not condoning that behavior in the least, but any guy with a brother knows what I'm talking about.

It's an unwritten rule-"I got your back no matter what."

Drinking was one of the few things we had in common.

We were two years apart in school, and although we had a few of the same core friends, we hung out with different crowds.

But when we drank, we were buds.

We were grown men who acted like a couple of teenagers when we were drunk.

As soon as we got to Weirs Beach, we gave all the kids a twenty dollar bill, and he and I hit the bar. I'd stand outside with Elle and Grace, and he'd be in the bar, doing a shot.

Then we'd switch.

When the kids came back about an hour later, we gave them another twenty.

This went on for another hour.

I lost count at ten shots each.

I don't remember anything else about that night.

After I was sober, and making my amends to people, my sister Andrea told me the story.

We came home around eleven that night and I didn't say a word to anyone.

Andrea, Kelli, and my mom were waiting for us.

I walked in and passed out on the couch immediately.

Drea said Elle, the dominant one, climbed on top of me and tried to cover me. She was trying to protect me.

Andrea said she's never seen anything like it.

It was like Elle knew I was in a horrible place and was trying to make sure I didn't hurt myself.

Grace laid on the floor below me, and both of them stayed there all night.

I jokingly asked Brian if he drove home the next morning, completely expecting him to say, "Yes."

When he said, "No, I thought you did," I knew I was screwed.

I knew things were getting out of hand.

I could take hiding the booze from my family. I had done it before, and would do it again.

One time I bought a half gallon of vodka to take to the cottage with me. I had it hidden in my duffel bag. If anyone were paying attention that weekend, they would've wondered why I kept going upstairs, every half hour on the dot, with an empty

Solo cup, but coming down with a full one.

My family had no idea.

I proceeded to drink a half gallon of whiskey that weekend too.

Every time I went to the bathroom, I'd sneak into the storage room, and take a swig out of my dad's gallon bottle. I knew the half gallon of vodka wasn't going to be nearly enough. So I helped myself to my dad's stuff.

I found out that he thought it was my brother-in-law who drank it all, and he couldn't believe anyone could drink that much in a weekend.

At the time I just nodded.

If he only knew it was me that drank it, along with a half gallon of vodka, I'm sure he'd be incredibly proud.

But the fact I had put my family and pups in danger (and Drea's *entire* family), the night at Weirs Beach, was something that completely scared and baffled me.

Was I getting that bad?

Was I drinking so much that I didn't even remember getting drunk?

I'd usually get buzzed, get drunk, get *really* drunk, nod in and out of a blackout, then pass out

This was new.

This was *I'm going to have a few, and then blank...*

I didn't care if I died.

But I wouldn't be able to forgive myself if I hurt someone else, especially my family.

My oldest nephew, who had his driver's permit at the time, told me later that he knew something was off when I drove over the middle of a rotary (roundabout) on the way home.

How I didn't kill us is something I'll never know.

The only thing I can attribute it to is that I almost have an automatic pilot that takes over when I black out.

I've driven home from Boston hundreds of times blacked out and never got so much as a scratch on any of my vehicles.

But this rotary was new. It had been installed the year before, and I wasn't used to it sober, never mind when I was blacked out.

So I drove over it.

After I made my amends to Drea, she asked me why the fuck didn't I give the keys to Bobby, her son, who had his driving permit.

I didn't have an answer for her.

None.

That was just the way my mind worked.

Or didn't work, in this case.

The thought never entered my mind.

And things just kept getting worse.

Towards the end of my drinking, right before I hit rock bottom, Liz asked me to go to her Father/Daughter soccer game.

She was in a traveling soccer league, and all the dads and daughters were going to play against each other. There'd be pizza and cake, and it'd be a great opportunity for the girls to bond with their dads.

I didn't want to go.

I knew if I went I wouldn't be able to drink.

And I didn't want to be anywhere where I couldn't drink.

What was the point?

I was so insecure and felt I had nothing to offer anyone in a social situation.

You mean I have to talk to other adults? I have to make small talk and look people in the eye?

No fucking way!

I couldn't possibly fathom how to do that.

The thought terrified me.

But it was important to Bella, and it was important to Liz, so I went.

Of course, being the diligent little alcoholic I am, I made sure I'd be at least buzzed.

Buzzed but behaved.

I had a few beers before we went, but knew that wouldn't be nearly enough, so I made a vodka and soda for the road.

But that wasn't going to be enough either.

I told Liz I wanted to get some gum, so my mouth didn't get dry playing soccer, so I stopped at a liquor store and bought four nips of Cuervo.

I drank two of them walking across the parking lot and drank one when I got to the soccer stadium.

I wasn't comfortable in the least but I just kept telling myself that people were not paying attention to me. They were there to play soccer.

I didn't embarrass myself, and Liz complimented me after, saying I played pretty well.

But that's not what bothered me.

I finished the fourth nip at halftime and felt such an overwhelming sense of emptiness when I threw the empty shot in the trash.

I needed more booze.

But how?

We still had a half a game left.

When I walked out of the bathroom, I saw a few of the mom's setting up a table full of pizza and other junk food.

And lo and behold, there in a tin tub, was seven or eight wine bottles, and an entire cooler full of beer.

I instantly felt better.

Ahhhh.

Somehow I held off until the end of the game, but I was the first one to the wine, and finished a few glasses before everyone came into the room.

Then I proceeded to drink as many beers as possible without seeming like I was out of control.

I didn't interact with anyone.

I didn't introduce myself.

Nothing.

I just wandered around, never making eye contact.

I was very good at looking occupied and busy in social settings.

But I was virtually unapproachable.

I got a few strange looks from a few of the

dads because of how fast I was drinking, but because I didn't appear drunk, they didn't say anything.

Little did they know I had had at least ten drinks since that afternoon.

What was even more disturbing, was that I was nowhere near drunk.

I was finally starting to feel "normal."

Most people would've been passed out by that point.

As the evening wore down (and I got drunker), the parents found me engaging and witty. But if I hadn't had anything to drink, I never would've said a word to any of them.

I remember in high school when I came up with the brilliant idea of dropping down a level so I could be in the same classes as the popular kids, a girl told me I was "The strong, silent type".

She was pretty, and popular, and unbeknownst to me, flirting with me.

I took it as a compliment at first.

Her boyfriend was the strong, silent type too.

He was older, and a Marine, and never said anything to anyone when he partied with us.

He was a badass.

So I decided I'd be a badass too.

What she didn't know was that I was terrified to talk to people. That's why I was so quiet.

I had nothing to say, nothing to offer anyone.

I was so insecure, I didn't even realize when a girl was hitting on me. It never entered the realm of possibility that I had something to offer the world.

It always bothered Bella that I never came out of my shell unless I was drinking. Whenever we went to her company outings or parties, she'd bring me up to speed on who bought a new house, who had a baby, who got a promotion, etc., so I'd have something to talk about.

She knew I was too shy to start a conversation on my own.

One time when I wasn't drinking there was a block party in our neighborhood, and she begged me to go.

I sat in the basement and played video games all day instead.

I was horrified to meet the neighbors.

She'd go for an hour, and then come back and tell me about this neighbor or that neighbor and how cool their house was or how cute their kids were, and ask me again to join her.

I didn't.

And because I couldn't swallow my pride or ego, I couldn't tell her that being in a social situation like that would paralyze me with fear.

So I gave her an attitude instead.

It killed me that I couldn't do something as simple as eat a burger with the neighbors for her, but I just couldn't.

Bella always believed in me. Always.

And she never gave up.

She always told me she saw moments of greatness in me, that she wanted her friends to see the person she saw when she looked at me, but that it was up to me to get out of my fucking way and live up to that potential.

But I never did.

Not when I was drinking.

Alcohol was calling the shots.

We were married in August of 2007, and it was a beautiful day.

I had spent the better part of the past year organizing the entire thing myself (Bella didn't mind and trusted me to do a good job), and it was all over in eight hours.

I remember sobbing that night after Bella had gone to sleep because it was over.

I tended to do that my entire life.

I was either dwelling on the past or planning for the future.

I never lived in the moment.

I had spent so much time and effort planning the wedding that when it was suddenly over, I became depressed.

I didn't even want to go on the honeymoon.

But I went.

I was so bloated from the three-day extravaganza of our wedding that I looked like a completely different person in the honeymoon photos. I was beat red and bloated, and I felt like my eyes were going to bulge out of their sockets from lack of sleep and dehydration.

We had a great time, and things were going amazingly well for a while.

We even got two golden retriever puppies the January after our wedding, and our little suburban family was complete.

But alcohol muddles everything.

Or at least it did for me.

I didn't communicate with Bella.

I stopped being sweet. I stopped being romantic.

We never addressed our issues.

My life was a very disciplined (albeit insane) day to day existence.

I'd get up, walk the dogs, run to the gym, work for four or five hours, start drinking around dinner time, home to walk the dogs again (and drink more), back to the house for dinner, stare at the TV (with a massive glass of wine next to me), then pass out.

That's what I did for the last three years of my drinking.

Every fucking day.

We couldn't make it work.

We tried various therapists, but I was too self-centered and angry to listen.

Or care.

The only thing I cared about was alcohol.

Chapter 9

Throughout my drinking, I went to detox three times.

The day I went to my second detox, I was sitting in front of my dad, with a half-empty bottle of Jose Cuervo in front of me, rocked off my ass, telling him I needed help.

I remember telling him I was lonely.

His jaw dropped.

"You? Lonely? You have an amazing wife, three amazing kids, and all the friends in the world, not to mention all of us."

He couldn't believe it.

But the truth was, I had been lonely most of my adult life.

I'd always had a void in my soul; a void that needed to be filled.

I guess that's what alcoholism is, to me anyway.

Something missing in my life, and booze was one of the few things that could fill it.

Of course, it wasn't filling anything.

It was just stopping me from feeling.

It was stopping me from growing and living

I never felt good enough.

People don't understand me (and never would). All these crazy, fucked up thoughts in my head are entirely unique. No one will ever be able to relate to me.

The void had always been there, but the further I got away from the innocence of childhood, the bigger the void became, the more lost and lonely I felt.

I remember watching M.A.S.H. with my mom, every weeknight at 7:30, back when we only had five or six TV channels.

Alan Alda's character was a surgeon during the Korean War, and in one episode he dreams he's in a little rowboat.

He's adrift on the water, and he sees all these prosthetic limbs floating around.

There are oars in the boat but he doesn't have arms, so he's just drifting. He's a doctor, and his specialty is putting people back together, and in the dream he's useless.

I was only twelve or thirteen when we watched that episode, but I never forgot it.

I felt the same way.

I felt lost and not able to do a damn thing

about it, years before I started drinking.

I don't remember anything specific about any of the three detoxes I went to, other than I blew four times the legal limit on the breathalyzer and the nurse looked at me and said, "You don't even look drunk."

Welcome to my world lady.

I remember the food being good too.

I gained over ten pounds each time. If I couldn't fill the void with booze, I was going to try to fill it with food.

But I didn't go to detox for me.

I went for Bella, and I went for my family.

I wasn't ready to stop.

I knew the only way I would stop at the end, during the last three years or so, was to be forced to do it.

Detox seemed like the way to go.

I'd get a break from work, it was covered by insurance, and my liver would get a rest.

There are a couple of things I do remember though.

We had to attend classes throughout the day to keep us occupied, and to help us see that there was a way out of our wasted lives.

During one class we were asked to write down the five most important things in our lives on five separate pieces of paper.

Then we were asked to throw all the little pieces of paper into a pile in the middle of the room.

The teacher looked at us, and told us that if we continued to drink and drug that we would lose everything in that pile.

Then he grabbed a few and read them out loud.

Kids. Money. Career. Wife. Health.

I didn't want to lose any of those things.

But I also didn't want to stop drinking.

Another thing I remember is meeting with my counselor during the second detox stint, and being completely baffled that I had ended up there again.

I told her I thought I was a sociopath because I didn't give a fuck about anyone, all I cared about was getting drunk.

I started bawling.

The counselor let me cry for a few minutes (I couldn't stop) and told me I was not a sociopath.

"Sociopaths have no remorse," she said, "do you feel guilty for what you've done?"

"Of course I do. Now. But I didn't even think

about who, if anyone, I'm hurting when I'm drinking."

"That's what alcoholism is Jay," she said, "you made the choice to pick up the drink, but it's the drink that takes you places you never would've dreamed of going."

It helped a little.

But not enough to stop me from drinking, probably because I didn't do anything as far as recovery was concerned when I got out of detox the first or second time.

I would behave for a few weeks and then felt like I deserved to drink, so I'd drink.

How I went nine months before we went to South Beach is a complete mystery to me.

The third time I got out of detox, I went to three meetings in two days but knew I was going to drink again.

I knew I was going to drink as soon as I checked myself out (against medical advice) because U2 was in town and I had never missed a local U2 show.

How's *that* for fucked?

I remember barely being able to drive to the stadium, and I purposely blew my friends off during the tailgate party because I was already kicked out of the house and knew it would've been written all over my face.

Better to drink alone.

I'll pass out in the Suburban after the show for a few hours.

I sat by myself too, complete with four nips of Cuervo in my pockets.

I don't remember much of the show, and have no idea how I managed to get back home to Brian's house.

I do remember blowing the second show off the next night though.

It was the first time in 20 years I had missed a U2 show in the Boston area.

I check myself out of rehab to see U2, knowing it was an insane choice, and then I'm too drunk and exhausted to see them.

I was falling, and I was falling hard.

For the next two weeks, I would drink more than I had in my entire life.

I lived on Brian's couch for the next twelve or thirteen days with a bottle of Jose Cuervo in one hand and a Coor's Light in the other.

I vaguely remember people coming and going

almost all day, every day, and the Showtime series "Weeds" was playing on a constant loop.

I was exhausted, but didn't sleep much.

When I passed out, I had no idea what time it was or what day it was.

I was stupid enough to drive to a 12-step meeting too, but I was drunk and had a nip or two in my pocket so I could go to the bathroom and chug it if need be.

I didn't eat unless Brian ordered take out, and forced me to eat something. Other than that he let me be.

At one point I went to Bella's house so we could explain to Joey that I was going to get help.

Joey was my buddy, and Bella thought he should hear it from me that it was a problem I'd be addressing.

I promised him I wouldn't drink anymore.

There's no way I would lie to a kid.

It didn't matter that I was drunk when I told him. I was telling the truth.

I was so sick of lying, so sick of hurting people, and so sick of drinking.

But the next thing I remember was that I was walking out of a liquor store with a pint of Cuervo and a twelve-pack of Coors Light in my arms.

I went home to Brian's and started drinking by myself, in my little boiler room bedroom.

I knew it wasn't working for me anymore.

My tolerance was so high it was nearly impossible for me to get drunk unless I drank as much as humanly possible, as fast possible.

There was no joy anymore.

No fun.

Nothing.

But I still kept drinking.

I couldn't stop.

Brian's friend's kept asking me to hang out with them in the living room, but I didn't.

A few of them knew I had been in detox the week before, and I didn't want to admit that I was already drinking again.

So I drank alone, and every once in a while I'd stumble upstairs to say hi.

As I brought the bottle of Cuervo to my lips for the last time, guzzling the last third of it in a few swallows, I was crying.

I never felt so desperate in my life.

That was October 3, 2009.

<u>Part IV: Redemption</u>

Wherever my story takes me, however dark and diffi-
cult the theme, there is always some hope and redemption, not because readers like happy endings,
but because I am an optimist at heart. I know the sun
will rise in the morning, that there is a light at the
end of every tunnel.

~Michael Morpurgo

Chapter 10

The morning after my last drink I woke up in my brother's boiler room with tears streaming down my face.

I wished I was dead.

If I'd had a gun there, I would've stuck the nozzle in my mouth and pulled the trigger.

Gladly.

I was done.

I couldn't do it anymore.

I crawled off the futon, walked through the kitchen, and pissed all over my brother's backyard.

I stumbled back to my room, and as I was about to lay down and pass out again for a few hours, I did something I hadn't done in almost twenty-five years.

In that nearly empty room, with the tiny swinging window carved high into the concrete and with the leathery aftertaste of Jose Cuervo stuck to my tongue, and stale, flat Coors Light rolling around in my gut, I got down on my knees, and prayed to a god I didn't believe in.

My prayer was simple, and I felt like a fool, but I did it anyway.

I need help.
I can't do this anymore.
Please help me.
Please.

Later that day I called a friend I had met at a meeting the previous week, and he told me to get him, and we'd go to a meeting.

As soon as he got in the truck, he asked, "Are you done?"

Without hesitation, I told him I was.

I got my 24-hour chip that night, and it was embarrassing and shameful, but I knew I had to do it.

Twelve-step meetings give out chips for various lengths of sobriety, and people consider the 24-hour chip the most important one.

If there's ever a time when someone needs to humble themselves, it's when they get that first chip.

So I did.

My friend insisted on it anyway.

Chips are also given out for 30, 60, 90 days, and sometimes they're given out for six and nine months too.

Once someone reaches a year of continuous sobriety, they receive a medallion.

I left my one-year medallion on the gravestone of Bill Wilson, the co-founder of Alcoholics Anonymous, tears streaming down my face as I did.

I gave my two-year medallion to a friend who asked me to be the one to present her with her 2nd-year-anniversary chip.

Of course, I said yes.

I was touched and humbled.

It's one of the highest honors in recovery, for me. And it's especially poignant when that person gives someone else that *same* medallion.

I gave another friend my four-year medallion when she reached *her* four years.

So I got my 24-hour chip that night, and thus began my journey in recovery.

I've been asked to get more in depth in regards to meetings, but I'm not going to.

It's an anonymous program for a reason.

I don't care who knows about my recovery (obviously), but I respect the program, and everything it stands for.

In the beginning, I went because it was

suggested I go.

I needed to kill time, there are over 2500 meetings a week in southeastern Massachusetts, and the meetings were a place where I didn't have to be alone.

It didn't necessarily mean I listened (I didn't) or that I was open-minded (I wasn't) to the solution many of them were talking about.

It was something to do.

The next few weeks were a haze, however, and I don't know how or why I stayed sober.

I think it was the fact that I knew I couldn't go back to the person I was.

I couldn't concentrate on anything.

I couldn't sleep, and I didn't eat much.

I felt completely lost.

I kept going to meetings, but I wasn't listening to anything that was said. When it was my turn to read, I'd pass, and I never spoke a word.

But I kept going.

The haze started to clear, but that made things worse.

Now I was starting to feel, and my emotions were all over the place.

I couldn't form a complete thought.

I was irritable, confused, and restless and didn't know what to do with myself.

At the suggestion of a friend, I started seeing a therapist, and that helped.

She didn't sugar coat anything, nor did she hold my hand, and tell me everything was going to be okay.

She told me what I had to do, and would ask the following week if I had done what she asked.

And she was a stickler for rules.

If I drank again, she wouldn't see me anymore.

It was that simple.

Exercise helped too.

I was feeling better physically, and it was during my workouts that all thought ceased.

I took solace in that.

It helped clear the cobwebs in my head.

I started thinking more clearly than I had in years.

I was finally sleeping better too.

My liver was starting to rejuvenate itself, and I wasn't dehydrated, but exercising made me feel better than I could ever remember.

I started getting up at 5 am to workout before

work (something I *never* imagined I'd do), and it was such a great way to start the day.

It was a great distraction too.

I had spent so much time drinking that I had a ton of spare time now.

Exercise occupied some of that time.

But I still didn't feel complete.

I still had that itch, that irritability.

I couldn't quite explain it, but I got angry at stupid, little things and I couldn't stand my boss.

I'd walk into work with an attitude, and look for any reason to go off on him if he did something to piss me off, which was often.

Then one day I told my boss I was going to kill him.

I was suspended indefinitely, and about two months later, when I was at our union hall checking my progress, I saw my termination letter on the union steward's desk.

It was also around the same time that the company was offering everyone an excellent retirement package. I asked my steward if I could retire instead of getting fired.

I would've eventually gotten my job back, but I was done.

Between my attitude and wanting a drastic change in my life, I said, "Screw it. I'll retire."

So I did.

I retired from a Fortune 500 company with great pay and benefits to pursue a career in fitness-something I knew nothing about.

Most people in my life thought I was insane, but I knew I was doing the right thing.

I knew that more than anything.

My dad was working for the phone company too, and I thought he was going to be more confused and disappointed than anyone.

The phone company offered job security for life, and I was walking away from it.

Then one day at my nephew's graduation party, he pulled me aside and said that he was unbelievably proud of me for going after my dream. He told me that he had always wanted to leave the phone company too, but because of his learning disabilities, he was afraid.

He told me it took great courage to do what I was doing.

I was floored.

Some people *still* don't understand my decision, and that's fine.

And some people have said that I gave up one addiction for another, and that drives me nuts.

I am *not* addicted to exercise.

I *am* addicted to alcohol.

When I start, I can't stop.

I obsess over it and keep drinking, even though I know it's slowly going to kill me.

And I'd go to any lengths to get it, including stealing spare change out of a co-workers Jeep to buy a few nips because I'd spent my entire paycheck (which I *did* and have since made amends to him).

I exercise for an hour a day, six days a week.

That's only 4% of my day.

When I'm done, I don't obsess, dwell or even think about exercise.

I live my life.

I don't lie, cheat, steal or hurt people when I'm exercising.

So there's quite a difference between my addictive alcoholic behavior, and my dedication and discipline when it comes to living a healthy lifestyle.

There are actually quite a few similarities between the 12 step program I belong to and exercise.

I've never left a meeting and felt worse.

I've never finished a workout and said, "Yeah,

that sucked. I'm so bummed I did that."

If I'm in a bad head space, both of them help me get my head on straight.

If I continue to do both on a regular basis, I have better results.

The further I get away from either of them, the further I get from being the best version of me that I can be.

I can't walk into a meeting and sit at the back and listen.

I can't walk into a gym and watch.

I have to participate in both.

And here's the most critical thing; once I *did* start seeing results, I *wanted* to keep going.

At the beginning, I went to meetings because I *had* to.

Now I go because I *want* to.

And if I don't exercise, I feel "off."

But I'm not obsessed with either of them like I was with drinking.

The twelve-step program I belong to is *not* my whole life.

Neither is exercise.

But both combined, especially when I'm consistent, help make my life whole. I can't describe it better than that.

But barring all that, my first year of sobriety was *still* exhausting.

I knew I didn't want to drink, but I had no idea what to do with my time.

My mind was always racing.

I couldn't sleep, and I convinced myself that if being sober was this tiring, I'd be better off drinking again.

At least if I were drunk, I wouldn't feel anything.

"Fake it 'til you make it," was one of the more popular slogans for newcomers.

Yuck!

I loathed most of those sayings when I first saw them.

But I kept going to meetings.

I went to work.

I exercised.

But I still felt like a zombie. And that was no one's fault but my own.

I was so afraid to talk to people.

I could never introduce myself, and when they'd introduce themselves, I'd said hi and keep walking.

It was suggested that I go to 90 meetings in 90 days.

So I did.

I was never told I had to. If that had been the case, I never would've gone to a single one. But I could take a suggestion.

I knew enough that if I drifted away from the program, and started isolating, I'd be *that* much closer to a drink.

I knew that, and I believed it with every ounce of my being.

So I took the suggestions that were offered.

I didn't take them all, but I took a few of them.

Luckily, that was enough.

At first.

I went to meetings, but I didn't listen.

I didn't understand the language, and I didn't understand how these people could smile and joke and be happy.

I fucking *hated* them for that.

How the fuck can you smile?

You're stuck in a church basement, drinking bad coffee, dying for a cigarette, and listening to Bob A. talk about how happy, joyous and free he is.

This is sobriety? Really? This is it? Are you fucking kidding me?

But I kept going, day after day after day.

Another suggestion was to *do* the work needed to stay sober, with someone of the same sex, for obvious reasons.

Addicts and alcoholics are lonely, lost, souls when they first put down the drink or the drug.

Some of us tend to choose new, unhealthy habits, and getting involved in a relationship is common as a newcomer.

So having a same-sex sponsor removes any of the drama or temptation that may arise. They're someone we can talk to if we were in a jam, someone with an unbiased opinion.

But, most importantly, a sponsor takes us through the 12 steps.

Of course, I didn't want anything to do with the 12 steps.

Isn't "God" mentioned eight times in that stupid commandment-like poster thingy hanging on the wall of every meeting in the world?

No thanks. I'm good.

I wasn't crazy about a sponsor either.

Some people put their sponsors on a pedestal,

and some sponsors can become ego-driven because of it.

But sponsors are no better or less than the person they're sponsoring.

They're there to take someone through the 12 steps.

That's it.

I learned one of my sponsors was a racist, homophobic, bi-polar, paranoid, sex addict after spending three hours in a car with him.

I learned that a guy from my home group, who I was hanging out with on a regular basis, had a crush on me.

He was a horrible father too, threatening to punch his kid in the face because he asked for a donut in the drive-thru lane.

I was sitting in the front seat when it happened.

It was also the last time I hung out with him.

I'm not judging anyone. I know both men were very sick.

They have since completed the 12 steps and have changed quite a bit (at least from my vantage point-which is from a distance).

But I certainly have no desire to spend any

time with them.

And that's okay.

My point is that when I walk into a 12 step meeting today, I'm aware of my surroundings. I'm more aware of how people act before and after a meeting, rather than what they say from the podium.

We are a sick bunch of people in those rooms.

And while going to meetings is an excellent start, we don't get better if we don't do the work.

Kind of like watching an exercise video, but not exercising. We simply won't get fit.

I joined a home group too.

The purpose of having a home group is for accountability, much like a personal trainer helps clients remain accountable.

The running joke is that you *have* to show up to your home group meeting every week and you can't miss it unless you're away or at a funeral-your own funeral.

There are "jobs" available within each group, and while it's not necessary to take a job, it's recommended.

Again, it comes down to accountability.

It may be something as simple as greeting people who come to the meeting, but it's a good way to stay connected.

My home group met every Thursday, and it was two blocks from my house.

No excuses.

But the main reason I liked it was because it wasn't in a basement.

The guys there were successful too. They wore suits and had nice watches and drove nice cars. They were well-spoken and well-groomed, but because my idea of a *real* alcoholic was a homeless guy, sitting in the gutter, drinking out of a paper bag, it lessened the blow that I was, in fact, a *real* drunk.

If these guys were drunks (and it took me months before I could say that out loud about myself), then maybe I wasn't as bad as a homeless bum.

I know now that I was being shallow.

Addiction affects everyone, and social status, income, race and/or sex have nothing to do with it.

Besides, my Thursday meeting *fit*.

It was as simple as that.

We could be more open because of the lack of women, and while some men just vented about their wives, most talked about their biggest fears and insecurities.

I could relate to these guys. I could under

stand what they were talking about.

It was such a relief.

I slowly realized that I wasn't alone, that the isolation and separateness I'd been feeling for most of my life wasn't unique.

That was enough to plant a seed, but I was still missing something.

The void was still there.

I felt stale and told my therapist as much.

She suggested I join a group that went on commitments to broaden my fellowship with other addicts, and alcoholics-to kind of force myself to build relationships.

Commitments were when a group would go to another meeting and speak. Sometimes it would be a regular meeting, and sometimes it would be at a detox or rehab.

I had been going to the same Monday night meeting for a few months because there was a cute girl there.

I walked into the kitchen after the meeting one night and asked to join the group.

The girl was there, with her mom, so I knew it was fate and that we were meant to be together.

But the thing that took me by surprise was

when the mom told me a bunch of them were going
out afterwards and that I should join them.

Huh?

*You guys do stuff outside of meetings togeth-
er? In public?*

What the fuck do you talk about?

*If it's only recovery talk, I'm all set. I go to
seven, sometimes eight meetings a week.*

*The last thing in the world I want to do is
talk about recovery at a restaurant.*

But I went.

I have no idea why, but I went.

That is something I would never have done
without being drunk, girl or no girl.

I wouldn't have.

But the amazing thing was, they didn't ask me
anything personal.

They didn't pry.

They didn't ask how long I was sober or what
my drug of choice was or what kind of wreckage I
had caused.

They accepted me for who I was.

There was a lot of goofiness, and a lot of
small-talk, and although I was entirely new, they
never once made me feel like an outsider.

I felt abandoned as a kid.

I felt almost invisible as a teenager.

As an adult, I was so lost and so full of alcohol that I had no sense of who I was.

But that Monday night, after almost thirty-seven years of feeling apart from everything, I was finally a part of something.

Chapter 11

Things went well for a while.

I was going to meetings regularly, going on commitments with my group, and I started to have a bit of a social life.

We'd all hang out after a commitment, usually going to dinner or someone's house.

We went on a few trips too, and the urge to drink never crossed my mind.

My workouts were going well, and I cleaned up my diet.

I always ate relatively healthy when I was drinking, but when you're drinking more than twelve drinks a day (and as many as thirty on some), it didn't matter. My liver and kidneys were working overtime trying to process all the alcohol.

I always had that fat, bloated look, like a sausage ready to burst.

I started to look healthy again.

And more importantly, I started to feel healthy too.

But even though I was active in my recovery group, and I was taking care of myself physically, something was still missing.

The commitments were always a good thing.

It felt like free therapy.

I was going on 4-6 commitments a week, and I spoke at most of them.

At first, I didn't know what to talk about so I'd recite my story.

It was boring and repetitive, but it helped me get out of my shell.

I also learned a ton about my group members.

It was such a good feeling knowing I could relate to them and their stories and they to me and mine.

I formed some of the best relationships of my life within my home group.

I can call almost any of them, still, to this day, even though I haven't been a member of that group for close to five years.

And I met a few people who taught me a few valuable lessons.

I learned to establish clear boundaries.

"No" is a complete sentence and I do not need to explain myself to anyone. Nor do I feel the need to lie if I don't want to do something.

A simple "No" will suffice.

If someone doesn't like it, that's on them. Their reaction to my decision has absolutely nothing to do with me.

I grew exponentially within my group. And I witnessed dozens of other grow too.

But something was *still* off.

I was angry a lot. And irritable.

I was doing everything I was supposed to be doing, and still, felt a little off.

A friend in the group suggested I do the twelve-step work.

No thank you.

Way too much God talk for me.

I'm all set with God and religion.

I had stopped believing in God twenty years before, and nothing was going to change my mind about it either.

I was raised Catholic, but both resented and didn't understand it.

Don't eat meat on Fridays.

No sex before marriage.

Homosexuality is a sin.

Did Jesus say those things?

I'm pretty sure he didn't.

I'm pretty sure he was a nonviolent revolutionary who hung around with lepers, crooks, and prostitutes; was anti-wealth, anti-public prayer, and anti-death penalty, but was never anti-gay, never mentioned birth control or abortion, never called the poor lazy, and never justified torture.

But the Catholic religion taught us to fear God, that He was a punishing God.

When we sinned all we had to do was go to confession, and we'd be absolved.

Yeah, that *makes sense.*

"Just say a few Hail Mary's, and you're good to go," the Priest would say.

So let me get this straight?

I can kick my brother in the shins or hide under my sister's bed when her friends are in the room, changing, and all I have to do is say an "Our Father" or two, and I'm good?

That's insanity.

And the damn church masses.

Are you kidding me?

It was the same mass every week.

I could say it verbatim by the time I was nine, complete with the chorus singers echoing "Hallelujah" when they sang *Our Father.*

It was dreadful.

I couldn't understand how these lemmings believed this garbage.

I've always had a bit of an attitude anyway, so when I was forced to do something, it drove me crazy.

I knew I had to do the obligatory stuff-make my bed, eat my veggies, do my homework, but having to do things like go to church, was asking me to have an attitude.

We had to go every Sunday, rain or shine, vacation or not.

I remember having to go to church at the lake.

Let's interrupt a perfectly good Sunday morning, stuffed into our "nice" clothes, and then go sit in a church that is not air-conditioned, for an hour, while everyone else is out on the lake, enjoying the sunshine.

Good times.

I didn't understand it, I didn't like it, and I never cared enough to ask questions.

I just wanted to be done with the whole thing.

When I was about to receive Confirmation ("accepting responsibility for your faith and destiny"), I told my mom I was an Atheist.

I told her that I didn't believe in anything and that it was contradictory to receive Confirmation when I didn't believe.

To my amazement, she agreed.

All I had to do was sit down with the priest and explain it to him.

So I did.

I convinced Brian to convert too.

I don't know how or when I got him on board, but I remember we were giggling when the priest came in the room, and the look from Mom was enough to burn a hole through steel.

From that day on I was an Atheist.

Mom insisted I was an Agnostic, that I believed in something.

But I didn't believe in anything at all.

Chapter 12

It's been stated that when a person starts drinking alcoholically, they stop growing emotionally and mentally.

I started drinking alcoholically when I was eighteen.

I stopped when I was thirty-six, but mentally I was still eighteen.

And it showed.

I had not one, but two chips on my shoulder.

I was angry.

I was defiant.

I was belligerent, irritable, short-tempered, and miserable to be around.

I knew something had to change or I'd im-plode.

I was a ticking time-bomb waiting to go off.

I was what we call a "dry drunk," and I know dozens of them.

Again, no judgment, but for me, being a dry drunk is worse than being an active alcoholic.

Our behavior can be every bit as insane and destructive as when we're drunk.

When I was drinking, I wasn't feeling anything.

My emotions were drowning under the drink.

But just putting the drink down wasn't enough.

Alcoholism is a three-fold disease; physical, mental and spiritual.

I had put the drink down, but I wasn't growing.

My emotions were at the forefront of everything, like a live wire inching dangerously close to open water.

Everything was electrified.

Everything was sharp and had angles.

It felt like the world's worst hangover when my head feels like glass and everything is annoying.

Everything is too bright, people smile too much, and I just can't quell my restlessness.

Loud noises set me off.

People being too nice set me off, or their laughter.

I hated happy people.

When I would walk into a meeting and see someone laughing, I wanted to strangle them.

What the fuck are you happy about?

This fucking blows.

My head feels like it's running a million miles an hour, my body is exhausted, but I can't sleep, and you're over there laughing?

What. The. Fuck!

Then I heard someone say, "You don't need to stop drinking forever."

Wait...what?

I don't?

"You just need to stop drinking for today."

BAM!

I just need to stop drinking today?

Hmmm....I can do that.

Why didn't I understand that years ago?

Again, it doesn't matter.

I could analyze it forever, but it wouldn't change anything.

What *does* matter is that things slowly started to fall into place.

People talk about spiritual awakenings all the time in recovery.

One of my first sponsors was notorious for simplifying things, and his definition of a spiritual awakening is as simple as "having a change in thought and attitude."

Alcoholics are a complete mess when we first

get sober.

  We don't walk into a meeting because we think it's a good idea, that it'll be a great time and a boatload of fun.

  Most alcoholics walk into a meeting because it's our last hope.

  Everything else has failed.

  And sometimes a spiritual awakening can be something as simple as identifying with another alcoholic or hearing something that clicks, as it did for me when I was told that I only needed to stop drinking for just one day.

Chapter 13

I was, however, fortunate to have a spiritual awakening that rocked my world.

I was at a meeting with the girl I was dating and her daughter.

Her daughter was restless, so I offered to take her for a walk until the meeting was over.

We left the basement, walked up the stairs, and when I tried the door to the central part of the church, it was open.

We walked in, and both of us were amazed at how beautiful it was.

I was thinking as much, but the three-year-old verbalized it.

"This is beautiful," she said.

What an odd thing for a little kid to say.

I agreed.

She grabbed my hand, and we walked further into the church.

Then I looked up at one of the stained glass windows.

It wasn't anything out of the ordinary and I can't describe it other than to say there was a figure of a man standing in the center of it. I may be able to point it out if I was in the church again, but that's about it.

I suddenly had an overwhelming feeling that something was in the church with us, that something was inside of me.

At first, I tried to shrug it off.

Dude...you watch way *too many movies. This will pass.*

You know it's just your imagination fucking with you?

Right??

I tried to shake the feeling, but it wouldn't go away.

It didn't get stronger, and it didn't change, but it was still there.

Something told me that it was there for me, that it always had been, and that it always would be, but that I needed to get out of my fucking way, and let it happen.

I needed to stop being so pig-headed and stubborn and selfish and maybe I needed to open my mind a little bit too.

Then, just like that, the feeling disappeared.

We left and returned to the meeting.

I wasn't going to share what had happened with the girl's mom, but I wanted to show her how pretty the church was, so I lead her back to the church proper.

The door was locked.

I don't know how and I don't know why, nor do I question it.

Someone from the church could've seen us leave the room and locked it behind us. Most church propers are locked when mass isn't in session, so that could've been that.

Maybe.

But I don' t question it.

Nor do I question that something touched me that day.

I have no idea what it was, but I know it was *something*.

I'm still not a Catholic. Nor do I practice any organized religion.

But I *do* know I'm not alone anymore.

And I probably never was.

One night after that day in the church Bella called me.

Grace was sick, and they were on their way to the vet.

I told her I'd be right there.

It was just before dawn and was still dark outside.

I immediately thought of the night Kelli was in her accident and suddenly felt on the verge of something, although I didn't know what it was.

When I got to the vet, Bella told me Grace was in the pre-op room.

She was heavily sedated because they were going to operate, but I wanted to see her anyway.

As soon as I walked in the room, I started crying.

My little Gracie, with her eyes droopy from the drugs, and looking completely confused, got up from where she was and stumbled over to me, trying to wag her tail and pulling her IV contraption behind her in the process.

I have never seen, heard or read about such an act of loyalty in my life.

Not even fucking close.

And that's when I lost it.

I sat down right there in the middle of the room and cried harder than I ever have as Grace crawled into my lap and rested her tired head on my knee.

All the pain I had felt for my entire life came to the surface, and I let it all go.

I let go of the confusion I felt when dad told me he and mom were getting divorced.

I let go of the abandonment I felt the night he left me in my bunk bed.

I let go of the anger I felt when I walked into a hospital room and saw my sister, my blood, crippled from the waist down.

I let go of the guilt I felt during my entire relationship with Bella, of all the hurt I had caused her and the kids.

I let go of the anguish I felt every time I put the bottle to my lips, knowing it was wrong and knowing I was killing myself but not having any idea how to stop.

I let go of the pride and ego that had been holding me back for as long as I can remember.

I let go of the fear that this sweet and loyal fur baby wasn't going to be with us forever and hoped that we had given her a great life because she deserved it.

She and Elle both deserved it.

But most importantly, I let go of the grief I was feeling over the loss of alcohol.

I knew I would never be able to drink again in safety, and it scared the hell out of me.

Alcohol had been my best friend all of my adult life, and I was so afraid to let it go.

But I knew I had to.

My therapist said that my relationship with alcohol was just like any other relationship, and that I had to go through the stages of grief before I could move on.

So I did.

I let it go as I sat on that cold concrete floor, cradling Grace, and sobbing like a child.

I couldn't stop.

Bella asked if I was all right and I couldn't answer.

The staff was starting to look concerned too, but I didn't care.

I held that sweet puppy in my arms, and I cried.

I was finally ready to let go of the insane grip alcohol had had over me for decades.

I knew I would never be able to conquer alcohol.

But I could surrender to it.

I knew I could do that much.

So I did.

I waved the white flag and let it all go.

The coldness (and close-mindedness) that had been surrounding my heart and soul for decades, slowly began to melt.

I finally believed that the world didn't revolve around me, that I wasn't alone, and the unconditional love that the pup in my arms (and her sister) had shown me since we brought them home one snowy night in January, was further proof that I was going to be okay.

I hadn't been sure of much in sobriety, but I knew, without question, that those two golden retrievers helped saved my life.

I was with a friend one night at the lake, just a couple months shy of my 8th year anniversary.

She had been gently (yet consistently) trying to get me to explain what sobriety was the entire weekend I was with her.

She wasn't trying to start an argument or de-bunk what I believed.

She just had a curious nature about her.

"Do the right thing," I answered finally.

"I'm not trying to oversimplify AA or the 12 steps," I continued, "but that's what it means to me.

"Do the right thing. All the time. Even when I don't want to, because that's usually when it's most important."

"But what about God and the spirituality part of it?" she asked.

"Come with me," I said.

I grabbed her hand, and we walked to a field behind the cottage I was renting.

It was a perfect August night, cool and breezy, and clear.

There were a million stars in the sky.

"Look up," I said.

She did.

She didn't say a word.

Neither did I.

After a minute or two, I broke the silence.

"I didn't create that."

She looked at me.

"I have no idea what did, but I didn't."

"*That's* what spirituality is to me.

"I didn't create that sky or those stars or the earth.

"I don't know what did, but I know it wasn't me. And that's enough.

"It doesn't have anything to do with religion or a god or anything like that.

"I simply choose to believe in something greater than myself. And I believe that whatever it is, helped get me sober.

"It helped me get my moral compass aligned again, pointing due north, which all comes back to doing the right thing.

"It all goes hand in hand."

She looked back up at the sky.

So did I.

"It can't be as simple as that, can it?" she wondered.

"It is for me," I said.

I'll never forget that day in the church, and I know it was a defining moment for me.

I'll never forget that day in the vet either. It was the most important and healthiest cry of my life-the most cleansing too.

But as an alcoholic, when simplicity is best (and often makes the most sense to another alcoholic), I relay the story about the stars in the sky on that grand summer night quite often.

Why?

Because it's the most natural idea to get my head around.

So many people get stuck when it comes to handing it over and asking for help from something greater than themselves.

Christ, I know I did (pun intended).

But having something else (no matter what it is) to rely on, is so freeing.

It's such a relief knowing I don't have to figure it all out myself.

After realizing that there *is* something greater than myself, I started to grow. The work I had to do in recovery wasn't easy.

But the steps necessary to leave my old life (and self) behind, and grow into the person I was meant to be, was simple.

It was all laid out in front of me.

All I had to do was follow a few simple suggestions, starting with admitting that I was powerless over alcohol.

I had done that a long time ago, the morning when I woke up crying and wanting to kill myself.

Now that I had a belief in something greater than myself, I could finally start to hand things over.

I could let go, surrender, and have faith that things were going to be okay.

Life would still throw its ups and downs at me, just like it does everybody, but now I didn't have to drink over it.

I could get through anything.

That was comforting, especially knowing I didn't have to go through it alone.

The people I met (and continue to meet) in recovery come from every corner of the world are not necessarily people I would usually hang with.

But the fact that we are all addicts and share that common bond of trying to make it through another twenty-four hours of sobriety, is comforting.

When I walk into a meeting, I instantly feel safe.

There's a beauty in that.

I used to try to analyze it.

How does this work? Why is it working? Why did it take two years for me to have a spiritual awakening? And why in a Catholic church, no less? Is that some sick, twisted joke?

I used to complicate everything.

And I used to try to control things too, namely people, places and things.

Then one day, I stopped sweating the small stuff.

I just went with the flow, accepted things for what they were (or weren't), and realized I have no control over anything in this world other than my actions.

I can't even control my thoughts sometimes.

But I *can* control my actions.

It's not always easy, and I often fail, but today, when I make a mistake or do something I shouldn't do, I have the knowledge to make things right, thanks to recovery.

I had to take a good look at myself when I started the 12 steps too.

That was hard.

To admit my character defects, my fears, my insecurities, and my resentments, and to put them down on paper, was exhausting.

And the list kept growing, the more I wrote.

But it was necessary for me to see it.

I needed to see where and what my shortcomings were.

Then I needed to share it with another person who had done the work before me.

I was ashamed and embarrassed to look at it on paper, so when I had to sit down with another person and share it with them, I was mortified.

But he didn't bat an eyelash.

He didn't say a thing.

He didn't gasp.

He didn't judge.

And even when I told him a few of the skeletons I promised myself I would never tell anyone, he related similar circumstances that he had been through.

I've never felt such a sense of relief in my life.

It was literally like that saying, "A weight has been lifted off my shoulders."

That's exactly how I felt.

I felt lighter. I felt free.

After I admitted all of my shortcomings, I had to be ready to have them removed.

That was a lot scarier than I thought.

I liked some of my character defects. I used a lot of them as defense mechanisms. They were part of who I was.

But I knew the parts of me that were less than desirable were a huge part of what was holding me back, self-centeredness and selfishness to name a few.

I still have most of my character defects. They're just a part of who I am.

But the difference now is that they aren't as transparent.

Now I have the tools to take a step back and to think the thought through before I let my defects surface and get the better of me.

I had to apologize to all the people I had harmed too. That was as humbling as anything I've ever done.

I remember driving home from Cape Cod one day, and I needed the phone numbers of two of my old bosses.

I called my dad and told him what I was doing. Then I called him back when I was done because it had dawned on me that I owed my dad an amends too.

Before I finished, we were both crying, and he

kept saying, "I'm so proud of you. Just keep doing what you're doing. That's all the amends I'll ever need."

If that isn't a power greater than myself working in my life, I don't know what is.

Keeping a daily inventory and checklist of my motives, praying to my higher power, and helping other alcoholics, are the last three steps, in a nutshell.

I won't dissect them all (and there is literature that does a *much* better job explaining it), but the last one is the most critical step for me.

Helping another alcoholic helps me as much as the addict I'm helping.

I'm able to relate to someone who's going through the same thing I went through.

It's also a reminder.

I go to beginner meetings because I *need* to hear the rawness of early sobriety.

I need to remember where I came from.

People new to sobriety are still very sick people, just like I was.

We put the drink down, but because alcohol or drugs were calling the shots for so long, we stopped being mature, responsible adults. Or some times we never grew up at all.

So we have to start fresh, from the beginning.

For me to be a part of that, to be blessed enough to be on their path (even for a brief time), and to see the light finally come on in their eyes, is the most profound and vital experience I've witnessed as a recovering alcoholic.

Chapter 14

My life is very simple now.

It'd be boring to some, but that's okay.

Today I'm happy.

I'm content.

I'm serene.

And most importantly, I'm comfortable in my skin.

I remember talking to my therapist one day, after six months of sobriety.

I was so sick of recovery, so sick of my life not changing, and so sick of owing people money.

I looked at her and said, "I've been sober for six months. Why is it so great to be sober? What's the pay off?"

"*Sobriety* is the payoff for being sober, you idiot," she answered.

And she was right.

If there's one saving grace for hitting rock bottom, it's that there is nowhere to go but up.

I'm one of the lucky ones.

Death wasn't my moment of surrender.

I was given the gift of desperation on October 4th, 2009, and changed my existence, in the best way imaginable.

Hundreds of thousands aren't as lucky.

There are 2.5 million alcohol-related deaths worldwide annually.

And I survived.

I don't know why and I don't question it.

I don't question a lot of things anymore.

Today I try to live my life, without expectation and judgment.

I wasn't judged when I walked into my first meeting.

Nor was I judged when I had to sit down in front of another man and tell him all of my darkest secrets.

When I had to make amends to the people I had harmed, almost all of them were completely understanding.

The one who wasn't is an active alcoholic who needs help himself.

Coincidence? Maybe.

It doesn't matter.

I did what *I* had to do.

I hope he gets the help he needs and I hold no resentment against him. It wouldn't matter if I did.

All that would do is block me from being the

person I was meant to be.

Today I can offer help to people who are still sick and suffering. I can offer them the suggestions I was given and help them. It scares the hell out of me, but I try to be of service as often as I can.

Every person I've worked with has gone back out and drank or used again.

All of them.

That destroyed my self-esteem and made me feel worthless.

Then one day I was at a meeting, and I shared what I was going through.

A woman assured me that I could *not* make anyone drink. Nor can I keep anyone sober. My only job was to guide them through recovery.

Then she mentioned that *I* was still sober.

I was floored.

Sometimes, at least for me, the most obvious things are so far out of reach they may as well be on Mars.

Bill W., the founder of the 12 step program I belong to, has a similar story.

He sponsored over 300 men during his first three years in sobriety.

Every single one of them drank again.

He was dumbfounded.

He was about to give up.

He said to his wife that it wasn't working, that it was pointless, and that he may as well drink again too.

"Bill," she said, "*you're* still sober."

Whoever said females are the fairer sex was onto something.

I can't change the past.

Nor can I worry about the future.

Today is all I have.

I know I'm not going to drink today.

I ask for help first thing in the morning,

I hang out with sober people, I exercise, eat right, and try to be of service to others.

And the urge to drink left me a long time ago anyway.

It's just not there.

I don't think about drinking, and I don't think about *not* drinking.

Alcohol was my best friend.

I couldn't exist without it.

I spent over twenty years in that relationship, and it took away everything I had.

It took away my dignity and grace and reason

and tact and integrity.

It took away my sanity.

I read the following excerpt somewhere on-line when I was about a year or two sober. And for the record, I have yet to be able to read it without sobbing like a baby:

One evening, an elderly Cherokee brave told
his grandson
about a battle that goes on inside people.

He said, "My son, the battle is between two 'wolves'
inside us all.
One is evil.
It is anger, envy, jealousy, sorrow, regret, greed, ar-
rogance,
self-pity, guilt, resentment, inferiority, lies, false
pride,
superiority and ego.
The other is good.
It is joy, peace, love, hope, serenity, humility, kindness,
benevolence, empathy, generosity, truth,
compassion and faith."

The grandson thought about it for a minute and then asked his grandfather:

"Which wolf wins?"

The old Cherokee simply replied,

"The one you feed."

I fed my wolf alcohol from the time I was fifteen until I was thirty-six years old.

And that beast thrived on it.

But today I feed it joy. And peace and love and hope and serenity and humility and kindness and benevolence and empathy and generosity and truth (even if my voice shakes) and compassion and faith.

I don't kid myself though.

Alcohol is cunning and baffling, and there have been millions of people who have relapsed and hundreds of thousands who never got sober again.

I know how dangerous it is to get comfortable in my sobriety. And if I were left to my own devices, I'd get very comfortable.

But that's not an option for me today.

Today I have help.

I have help every time I walk into a meeting.

I have support every time I pick up the phone

and call one of the handful of people I can say any-thing to. I have help when I practice what I've learned in recovery.

I don't know why I felt so alone for the first half of my life.

It doesn't matter.

Today I'm not alone (and never have been).

It took waking up in my brother's boiler room, with tears almost choking me, and the desire to die so strong that I would've done anything to stop feeling the pain I felt, to realize that I was done.

And that I needed help.

So I got down on my knees and prayed to a god I didn't believe in.

I didn't hate him, and I wasn't angry at him.

I just didn't believe.

A few years later I was telling this part of my story to a doctor from Montana.

He said, "Your prayer was answered."

I stood silent for a minute, just staring at him.

I couldn't get my head around what he had just said.

The thought had never occurred to me.

"You're right," I finally said, "it was."

———————————

My life has turned around in ways I never thought possible since I became sober.

Today I can be an uncle and a son and a brother and a friend.

I'm kind today.

I'm polite and sweet, and I have tact and grace and integrity.

Today I can be trusted.

Today I can be counted on.

Today I don't lie.

And today I always try to put others first.

That doesn't mean I sacrifice what I need to do for me. It means because I *do* put my sobriety first, I can be of service to others.

Today I have a roof over my head, food in my belly, clothes on my back, my health, and my sobriety.

And every day I'm thankful for those things because it's a lot more than what some people have.

Since I've been sober, I have my family back in my life.

I have a few close friends that I can share anything with, and they'll never judge me.

I've been able to go back to school to get a certificate in both personal training and nutrition.

I've made arrangements with my debt collectors, rather than ignoring the phone calls and letters.

Bella and I are friends.

I can be there for her kids, and although I was an active alcoholic for most of their childhood, I am unbelievably proud of the people they've become. I'm simply *beaming* with pride for them.

Bella always said she saw moments of greatness in me and I like to think that every once in a while a few of those moments shined through when I was with the kids.

I hope that I played a small part in the people they've become.

Rae graduated from a New York college and lived in Brooklyn for years, loving the Big Apple life. She's now in Oakland with her boyfriend, crushing it in her respective industry.

Liz is soaking up the sun in California, and her courage inspires me every day-more than she'll ever know.

She went out to Loyola as a freshman, and as of this writing, has almost four years sober herself.

I've seen her speak at meetings, seen her sing

in nightclubs, and most importantly, I've witnessed the woman she's become, thanks to recovery.

I still see Joey almost daily, and although I'm biased, every single person who knows him can attest to the fact that he's one of the best people around.

I wrote this book too.

I've always wanted to be a writer.

I went to school and majored in English years ago, but never finished.

I took several online writing courses and was published in a magazine.

But alcohol always got in the way.

But not anymore.

Not today.

Today, if I continue to do the right thing and ask for help when I need it, I know I can do anything I put my mind to.

And today I realize that there is *always* something to be thankful for.

Always.

I never forget that.

I didn't die from alcoholism. I didn't become homeless or sick or hurt or kill anyone.

I lost everything that makes me who I am, including my sanity, but thanks to sobriety, I was able to find all the important things again.

I was able to become human again.

Back in 2011, I volunteered at The Wilson House in Vermont.

The co-founder of Alcoholics Anonymous was born there.

I promised myself I'd volunteer at least twice a year and when I was a few months sober, I spent the weekend.

When I found out they were looking for volunteers, I signed up for a two-week stint.

The day I got there I noticed signs all over the inn that said, "3-Month Volunteers Needed."

I don't believe in coincidences anymore. Good, bad or indifferent, I believe everything happens for a reason.

So after my two weeks were up, I went home, spent Thanksgiving with my family, and told them I was moving to Vermont for three months.

I became the live-in innkeeper of The Wilson House on December 1st.

I was responsible for tending to guests needs, doing light cleaning, helping in the kitchen during Friday and Saturday night dinners, stocking the fire wood, and taking care of two goats, a handful of chickens, and Barley, the house golden retriever.

Barley and I were the only ones in the inn on most weekend nights, and I'd be lying if I said I didn't hear or see a few things that spooked me a little.

The dishwasher turned on by itself one night.

I was in the front office and went into the kitchen as soon as it happened.

There were no guests in the house, and the back door was locked. The front door was to the right of the office, so no one would've been able to walk in without being seen.

The same thing happened the next night.

It turns out the dishwasher was set on a timer and automatically goes on three hours after its last use.

A few days later the top drawer in the office desk opened as I was sitting next to it.

The desk drawer had a faulty latch, and opened more than once when several of us were in the room, but it was eerier when I was by myself after dark.

But one night, when I was lying in bed, I heard footsteps walk past my bedroom.

There were no guests and Barley hadn't been

upstairs in years, due to his age.

I thought it was the owner of the inn (she lived down the street) because she had an office next to the back staircase.

It was a little odd that she'd be out at 1 am but what freaked me out was that the footsteps stopped just beyond my room.

I didn't hear them walk down the stairs and I didn't hear them walk into the office.

Nor did I hear them walk back down the hall, the way they had come.

They stopped right outside my room.

And although I never heard them again, I wasn't afraid that night.

Maybe it was Bill W., coming for a visit, checking to see how I was holding up.

Who knows?

What I do know is that those three months in Vermont were some of the best times of my life. And they certainly solidified the most spiritual part of my recovery.

There were different seminars every weekend, and I was allowed to take part after my chores were done.

There was at least one meeting a day, and

sometimes as many as three.

All the volunteers were in recovery too, so even when we were hanging in the kitchen or out on the porch (complete with rocking chairs), we'd always be talking about recovery.

I met people from all over the world and have a few life-long friends because of it, not to mention that this particular spot in Vermont is one of the most serene places I've been to.

My friend's mom (who transplanted there from New Jersey) said it best when she said, "I love this valley. Every time I leave and come back home, it feels like the mountains are embracing me in a warm hug."

I couldn't agree more.

The inn is about seven miles from a quintessential New England town (complete with a two-screen movie theater), and I'd spend my day off at the local bookstore.

There was also a gym just outside of town so each morning after breakfast I was able to tend to the physical aspect of my recovery

All the areas of my life (physical, mental, spiritual) were being taken care of, and I loved it.

It was the first Christmas without my family.

But they understood and were happy for me.

They missed me, but knew I had to do this for me.

We had a small dinner and then we sat around the fire, talking about recovery and what it meant to be sober.

And although I've had many wonderful Christmas's with my family, the one in Vermont will always stand out.

It wasn't about presents, and it wasn't about endless weeks of preparation.

It was about a few recovering alcoholics enjoying a meal, and helping each other stay sober for one more day.

Those are just a few examples of the gifts I've been given in sobriety.

Today I have focus and purpose.

When things get overwhelming, I'm able to take a step back, assess the situation (and I usually do that by running any significant decisions by other people in recovery) and approach the problem head-on, and rationally.

That's huge for me.

I used to be so reactionary. For me, my first thought was usually the wrong one (and the one that would get me into the most trouble).

But today I've done (and am doing) things I've never imagined.

In 2013, I drove 9000 miles across the country and back in an RV to promote fitness.

Financially, it was the most irresponsible thing I've ever done because I didn't have the money and had to borrow it from my family, but it was one of the most amazing things I've ever done.

Again, I was flying by the seat of my pants (something I continue to do, although it's with much less frequency).

I rented an RV I couldn't afford and took off on a 9000-mile journey-solo, no less.

I convinced myself I'd be able to raise enough money along the way, to pay for gas, food, and any incidentals, as well as building my multi-level marketing business as I went.

I ran out of money by the time I reached Utah, roughly two weeks into a six-week trip.

The point of the trip was to stop in every major city along the way and to give a free workout to whoever wanted it.

I'd give a brief introduction to the benefits of exercise, share my story, and then tell them how I

took my health back (through the multi-level market
ing company I was representing).

We'd work out, everyone would feel great,
and they'd sign up under me.

I'd be wildly successful and live happily ever
after.

Not one person signed up, nor did anyone
buy any of the programs I was so passionate about.

And because I didn't do enough research,
renting the RV proved exponentially more expensive
than it if I had just stayed in hotel rooms along the
way.

The gas alone for the RV was over $4000.

Mom came to the rescue and wired me cash
and sent me her credit card (*just in case).*

I had to use it by the time I left Los Angeles to
head back to Boston, but I'm also happy to report
that I've paid mom (and Kelli) back every penny I
borrowed (well over $10,000).

That's where my mind goes when I'm not
thinking clearly: *I want what I want, and I want it
now.*

It's dangerous and impulsive.

I was behaving like I did when I was drinking,
even though I wasn't drinking.

I drove to New Jersey one night because I was bored and had met a girl at Staples the previous week.

We exchanged numbers, and suddenly I'm driving to her house, 250 miles away.

I called her, she answered. I told her I was in Connecticut, and that I'd be at her house in three hours.

I slept on her couch for the next two nights and then left because it was Christmas Eve and I knew I had to be with my family the next day.

We're still very good friends (just saw her on a business trip to California) but that's how impulsive I can be.

I have since learned that I should probably talk to my sponsor (or one or two other trusted people in recovery) *before* I make any major decisions in life, including spontaneous road trips.

But I met dozens of amazing people on my Drive4Life cross-country trek.

They were extremely kind to let me into their homes and to spend a day or two with me, often sending along care packages of toiletries and snacks for the road.

I'm in contact with almost all of them on

social media, and I love witnessing how their lives are unfolding, even if it's from a distance.

I was able to see this country of ours too, and I'm *still* amazed at how unique the people and land-scapes are.

It's like we have hundreds of little worlds spread out all over this nation.

It was exhausting to drive that distance by myself, although I did have a friend help me drive for four days from Chicago to Denver (love you Johnie!) and although I'm not sure I'd ever do it alone again, I'd do in a heartbeat with a few friends.

This country is beautiful. And awe-inspiring.

I'm grateful I live here, and I'm thankful I was able to take that trip.

And of course, I went to meetings along the way.

I went to a meeting just down the road from Notre Dame University, where two big, burly guys took me out for a steak dinner after the meeting. One of them was from a town just north of Boston.

I went to a meeting in Denver where we sat on couches in a candlelit room.

I went to a meeting in Reno where the

average age was 84, and the temperature was even higher.

I went to a meeting in Austin where the first speaker had us laughing so hard, I felt bad for the second speaker, knowing he couldn't possibly relay his message of experience, strength, and hope with such passion and humor.

And I was right.

But his story was every bit as compelling and powerful, and most of us were crying as hard as we had laughed at the first gentleman.

I went to a meeting in West Virginia, where I was beyond physically and mentally exhausted.

Bella's mom had been battling cancer, and we knew the end was near.

At that point, I just wanted to be home.

I stepped outside after the meeting, and saw one of the prettiest sunsets I've ever seen.

And I'll never forget it.

I'm tearing up as I type this (and I'm tearing up *again,* as I'm rewriting it four years later) because, well...because that's just how fucking cool sobriety is.

I stood at the top of the tallest building in North America in Chicago, and I stared in wonder at the St. Louis Arch, wondering how the hell they made it.

Outside of Denver, I goofed around (and tried to film a fitness video) at Red Rocks Amphitheater.

It was rainy and raw when we got there, and we were exhausted from driving twelve hours straight through Kansas the night before, but it was beautiful and sunny by the time we left.

At Estes National Park, elk the size of moose roamed around the center of town, like squirrels roam around Boston Common. We hung out at the Stanley Hotel, which was the inspiration for Stephen King's *The Shining*.

The Rocky Mountains took my breath away as I was driving from Denver to Wyoming.

I was on I25, driving north, and when I looked to my left, I noticed a mountain range. Then I looked again and saw another set of mountains, this one higher than the first. When I looked a third time, I gasped because what I thought were clouds were, in fact, an even higher range, covered in snow.

I've never witnessed something so powerful before.

And while I've had one or two women take my breath away, a landscape never did. That is until I saw the Rocky Mountains.

I picked up a hitchhiker in western Colorado.

I kid you not, his initials were J.C, and yes, he was wearing sandals and had a beard.

He asked me to drive him to Seattle, but after discussing the importance of weed (and telling me he had a knife stashed in his bag), I politely declined.

I dropped him off at a gas station and drove east, sixty miles in the wrong direction, so I wouldn't have to drive by him as he was walking up the expressway entrance ramp.

The California coast is as majestic as anything I've ever seen, and Big Sur, in particular, feels like something out of a J.R.R. Tolkien book.

Arizona is hot and much lusher than I had pictured (so is Tennessee-it's so green!) and Texas is enormous.

The night I landed in Austin I sat down in a cafe, ordered a tea, and Michael Jackson's "Don't Stop 'Til You Get Enough" came on.

There were only a handful of patrons and a few staff in attendance, but every single one of us started grooving.

And I don't dance.

But I did that night.

Because that's just how fucking cool Austin is, that's just how fucking cool sobriety is.

I cut the trip short because Bella was keeping me updated on her mom's condition and it was getting worse.

I drove over 1200 miles through the night aided by massive amounts of caffeine, stopping only for a few hours of sleep in New Jersey.

I woke up because something didn't feel right.

Five minutes later I got a text from Bella, saying her mom had passed.

I was home four hours later, knowing Bella would've done the same for me.

It was a great feeling knowing I could be there for her when she needed someone.

For *once*.

For me to *finally* be able to do something for her, without any hidden agenda, was such enormous growth for me.

She knew it too, but was still a little surprised when I showed up at the crack of dawn in a dusty RV, looking like I hadn't slept in days.

I hadn't, but she didn't need to know that.

It was about being there for her.

So I was, because of what I have been taught

in recovery.

That's the best thing about sobriety-when I put others first, I know it's the right thing to do.

It's not always easy, and sometimes I don't *want* to do it, but when I do, everything falls into place.

I never would've taken that trip across the country when I was drinking. I would've talked about it, but I never would've done it.

But I did.

Chapter 15

Since the first edition of the book, the response has been overwhelming.

I knew that the book wouldn't keep anyone sober (nor would it make anyone drink) but if someone could relate to (or identify with) what I had gone through, maybe they wouldn't feel so alone.

But the one thing people mentioned, more than any other, was that they wanted to know more about where I am *now*.

I touched on my life in sobriety in the first edition, but four years have passed since then, so I decided to add a few chapters to expand on what continued sobriety is like.

It's nothing earth-shattering.

There's no secret.

I'm not wildly successful.

I still have debt.

And I still live one day at a time.

The only difference between now and then is that it's even *more* important to stay connected and to keep doing the work.

I can't stress that enough.

I've been to two funerals of heroin addicts

who thought they had one more relapse in them.

Boston is riddled with an opiate epidemic, and I see people mourning friends and loved ones on social media on an almost-daily basis.

I know a woman who went back out after twenty-five years, and I've heard of a gentleman who went back with more than forty years of sobriety.

He left his 41-year medallion on the bar after ordering a drink, didn't say a word to anyone, and walked out into the night.

No one has heard from him since.

I ran into a friend when I was seven years sober and he had over twenty. He was doing great, and I was so happy to reconnect with him.

Two nights later I ran into him again, and he told me his brother had just died from a drug overdose.

He said his family didn't understand why he was at a meeting, considering the circumstances.

His response: "Jay, I need to be here. Someone may need my help."

And that's precisely the kind of people I try to emulate.

It's also why I chase my sobriety the way I do.

I see people on a daily basis who get away

from doing the right thing and quickly morph into a miserable, dry drunk. They stop going to meetings, they fade into the background, and they stop answering calls or texts.

I know it's just a matter of time before they come back, after going out (if they're lucky), their heads tilted in shame.

And *every single one of them* says the same thing:

It's not any better out there. It's just as bad. But now it's worse because now I have a head full of recovery and a belly full of beer. I thought I could control my drinking again. I was wrong.

Today I try to surround myself with people who are *only* going to lift me higher.

I know that sounds arrogant or that the people in my life are "better than" others, but it goes back to believing there are merely only two types of people in the world; those who get it and those who don't.

I have no problem with the ones who are *trying* to get it (and most of them usually do, if they apply themselves a bit) but I can't waste energy on people who refuse to change and grow.

I don't hate them, think less of them, or

wish them any ill will.

There's zero judgment either.

I was lost for decades. I've been in their shoes.

But I know what I need to do for me and my recovery.

I remember when I was two years sober and I started hanging out with a group of newcomers, all with less than six months of sobriety.

It was dramatic and exhausting, and quite simply, it was toxic.

My sponsor noticed I was off. He told me that he *never* hangs out with newcomers (he'll work recovery with them though), but tries to hang out with people who are on the same level as him.

It made sense.

So I establish clear boundaries, wish newcomers the best, and move on.

It's not my job to save everyone or even *any*-one.

I can help people, offer suggestions, and listen, but it's not my job to be anyone's taxi service, bank, marriage counselor or landlord.

One of my most prominent character defects is my lack of assertiveness.

I'm a people-pleaser by nature.

I hate hurting anyone's feelings. But there are a lot of sick people still out there, people who don't have any concept of boundaries.

I've had people ask if they could move in with me and I've had people ask if I'd come to the west coast to take care of them.

I had one woman ask me if I'd pay her hotel bill in Chicago because her air conditioner was broken and it was hot, and she had to take her kids to a hotel to keep them cool, and she could pay for the room with her credit card but needed cash for food.

Ummm...fuck no!

And my response was just that, although I didn't swear.

It was a simple, "No."

I didn't need (nor want) to give her any explanation beyond that one word.

Like I said before, "No" is a complete sentence.

And it is.

When I heard that in a meeting, it was like I was slapped in the face. And it was said by someone I didn't think I had anything in common with, no less.

It was almost paralyzing when I tried to say

that (and nothing else) in the beginning.

But it became easier and more natural the more I practiced it.

And other people's reaction to me saying "No" has absolutely nothing to do with me. That part is on them. I'm establishing clear boundaries from the get-go.

Today, I'm *still* doing what I was doing when I first got sober.

I still go to meetings.

I still talk to my sponsor.

I still actively work the steps. I'm currently going through them again, for the third time, just like I did years ago.

Granted, it's a quicker process, and not so mentally exhausting, but it's important to keep doing the right thing. And I learn something new every time I reread things I've read hundreds of times.

I'm still being as open-minded and accepting as before too (hopefully even more so, because of what I've been taught).

I still have bad days.

I still have incredible days.

But most of my days are even-keeled.

And I need that.

I've had amazing things happen to me since the first printing of this book.

I witnessed my younger sister have her third baby (with a fourth on the way), and while I didn't think it was possible to reach a higher level of awesomeness in parenthood with each passing kid, she continues to do just that.

I moved to one of the greatest cities in the country.

I was living in a very toxic household for the first five years of sobriety, and it became too much.

I hated going home and avoided it at all costs.

I was living with three active addicts, and my group members couldn't believe my living conditions.

I reached out to my dad and asked him if he could keep his ears open for an apartment or maybe a friend of his had a room in their basement.

The next day he called and asked me if I wanted to live in his childhood home, the one he still owned with my aunt, but which was now vacant because my aunt was in a nursing home.

Of course, I said yes.

The house is old, and in dire need of a cosmetic upgrade, but living in the house my dad and grandparents lived in is comforting.

It's going to take a while for me to get my finances strong enough to buy a house of my own, but I'm okay with that.

I'm not ashamed of it.

It's just who I am.

I destroyed my credit when I was an active alcoholic, but I've slowly been chipping away, and it's getting better.

I know how unbelievably blessed I am to have a roof over my head.

And I get to live there alone.

It's my little sanctuary.

I could care less that the aluminum siding is pink or that there's paint peeling from the ceiling (I think it gives the house character).

And I love the neighborhood too.

There's nothing quite like a Dorchester neighborhood.

Cops and firefighters surround me, and I live on a small, one-way street, so traffic is non-existent.

When I'm traveling, the neighbors take my trash in, and there have been numerous times when I've come home and not only is *my* sidewalk plowed, but the *entire* street is clear of snow.

I'm still writing.

I probably don't do it as much as I should, but I'm currently working on a few things.

I "acted" in a major motion picture (as an extra) alongside Batman and although I have no aspirations of being a Hollywood star, it was a very cool experience.

I've been able to see U2 several times in sobriety.

That may not seem like a big deal to some, but it's a huge deal to me.

The first time I saw them, I was a fourteen-year-old kid who hadn't taken his first sip of alcohol yet, and it was the best (and first) concert of my life.

Seeing them sober now, is almost as special as it was 30 years ago because I'm present in mind, body, and soul.

My youngest sibling got engaged this past summer.

My dad celebrated his 80th birthday this year.

I was a guest speaker on a podcast about addiction and recovery.

My nephew graduated from Wentworth College in Boston, and I witnessed it.

I was asked to speak at an awards dinner in my hometown.

I took my first drink in Braintree. I took my last drink in Braintree. And I spent the first five years of my sobriety in Braintree.

So, of course, I said yes, without even thinking about the impact of it.

I had come full circle, and it was one of the most poignant things I've ever been a part of.

I received my 6th, 7th, and 8th-year medallion since the first edition of this book.

When I was working in Connecticut, I was in a meeting, and ran into a gentleman who had volunteered at The Wilson House when I was there.

He was a significant influence on me, and although he loaned me a book (which I *did* return), I never thought I'd see him again.

In all the gin joints in all the world.

And then he comes walking into the Connecticut meeting.

That's just how recovery works.

No coincidences.

But things aren't always perfect in sobriety.

I have to live life on life's terms, and sometimes life throws us curveballs.

It's knowing when to swing that makes the difference-or more accurately, when to hand it over to something greater than myself.

I learned I was born with a heart defect a few years ago.

I have a bicuspid aortic valve, while the rest of the world has a tricuspid valve.

My valve has to work overtime, and because of it, blood is regurgitated into my lungs.

I may have to have open heart surgery at some point (and it scares the hell out of me), but I'm taking that one day at a time too, just like how I take everything.

I now have reading glasses, my back is getting worse the older I get (arthritis in my L4 and L5), and I have to limit my exercise (no isometric exercises, no heavy lifting, and no contact sports).

I know that those things are all just age-related, but sometimes I get a little spiteful.

Sometimes I feel like I'm just getting started, regarding who I am, what I want to do, and who I want to become.

And I don't want anything slowing me down.

But my friends always remind me that there is always something to be grateful for.

And I agree.

On December 10th, 2017, we were told that Grace had a month to live because of inoperable nasal cancer.

On January 4th, 2018, I laid down and spooned the prettiest blonde I've ever known and whispered in her ear, telling her over and over how much I loved her and how she had saved my life.

It was, by far, the hardest thing I've ever had to do.

But not once, from the time we heard of Grace's cancer, until she took her last breath in my arms, did I think about drinking.

In the past, I'd drink over everything.

I'd drink to make the pain go away. I'd drink when I was sad, and I'd drink when I was lonely.

I was all of those things for Grace's last month on earth.

But not once, not even for an instant, did I think about drinking.

I didn't think about it when I was sobbing after the news, and she was licking the tears from my face. I didn't think about it when we had the home visit scheduled, but canceled at the last minute because we just weren't ready. I didn't think about it when I took her on her final walk, the snow falling around us and sprinkling her coat with flakes of white, knowing how much she loved being outside in a storm.

And I didn't think about it when her body went limp against mine, as I laid spooning her and whispered in her ear.

Drinking never entered my mind.

Not once.

And that's because a sweet, gorgeous golden saved my life and loved me unconditionally when I couldn't love myself.

Elle was lost for weeks afterward, and so was I, but we got through it together, and Bella and I spent more time with Elle than ever before.

I still miss Grace every day, but I know we did the right thing and that she's in a better place.

And I'll see her again someday.

I know that too.

Chapter 16

After becoming a Certified Personal Trainer with The National Academy of Sports Medicine, I worked at several high-end gyms and learned very quickly how similar they are to any other corporation in the country.

All they care about is about making money and selling, and while I'm all for the former, I'm not a salesman. I had to sell myself by constantly pestering the gym members, and it simply isn't my style.

The hours were long, the pay was deplorable, and the false promises I was told upon being hired at each, were glaring.

I became friends with some of the most knowledgeable trainers I've ever met, and I loved that aspect of it. Continually learning new things about health and fitness from different perspectives was both fascinating and informative.

But the entire scene just wasn't for me.

I started Ubering part-time towards the end of my training career.

It was a no-brainer.

I could work when I wanted to, as much as I wanted to, and I could stop at any time, simply by shutting the app off.

Knowing Boston really well certainly helped and I've always loved to drive.

It certainly isn't lost on me that the majority of my clientele are either buzzed or drunk.

I pick up drunk people all the time.

And of course, college kids reeking of weed, are a regular occurrence.

But it's my job to get the passenger home safely, and I take pride in that.

I know these people have families, and loved ones, and it's my job to get them where they need to go.

I had two heroin addicts in the backseat one early summer day in 2018.

When I pulled up, I noticed a sleeve of tattoos on the tall one, most of them from prison.

The shorter one snubbed his cigarette on the ground and put the stub back in his pack.

Heroin addicts do everything in slow motion.

They talk slower and move slower, almost as if they're underwater.

They even blink in slow motion.

Judging by their movements, these two had shot up minutes before.

We talked about my car (they were impressed it was so sporty), the Patriots (Tom Brady is a semigod in Boston) and traffic (always a favorite topic).

The one behind me nodded out, and the taller one was on the phone with a friend, telling him he had just scored and that he was on his way home.

Their conversation turned towards Long Island, a detox located in Quincy, a suburb directly south of the city that touches Dorchester.

It's in Boston Harbor, accessible only by bridge, and several scenes from "Shutter Island," were filmed there.

It's one of the creepiest places I've ever been to, especially when it's rainy and windy, and *every* time I was there, it was rainy and windy.

"I've done commitments out there," I interrupted when the kid hung up the phone.

"Oh," the one who had nodded out woke up and piped in, "you in recovery?"

"I am," I answered.

"How long you been sober?" the other asked.

"A little over seven years."

"Damn man. That's awesome. Good for you," Sleepy said.

"Thanks," I said, "it takes a little work, but it's

a pretty good way to live."

They were quiet.

The one behind me nodded out again.

The other one made another call, and let the person on the other end know that they got the stuff.

The subject of recovery didn't come up again.

We were silent the rest of the ride.

I pulled up to their house.

They thanked me.

Then they walked across the street to stick a needle full of poison into their arms.

Again.

A few weeks later I picked up two kids at a sober house in South Boston.

I told them I was in recovery, and for the next twenty minutes, the three of us had a mini-meeting in my car.

The one behind me had just got his six-month sobriety chip, and the other one had just received his one-year medallion.

I asked them if the sober house was working

for them, if they were doing what they were supposed to be doing, and if they were doing okay.

They replied "Yes" to all three.

"It's crazy though," the one behind me said, "we had a kid die of an overdose last week in the house. No idea how he got the stuff [drugs] in, but he died lying on his bed."

"This fucking drug [heroin] is killing us, man," the other one said, "how the fuck do you overdose in a sober house?"

"If we want to use, we always find a way," I said, "some people tell themselves they can go back out and that one time ends up being the last. That's addiction."

When I pulled up to their address, I recognized it.

I wasn't dropping them at a crack house or a heroin dealer's apartment or a back alley so they could score.

I was dropping them at a 12 Step meeting.

I got both of their names, introduced myself, and told them that maybe I'd see them around, in the halls. I drove away with hope in my heart that night, but not before saying a little prayer for the sick and suffering still out there.

I became a Recovery Coach/Sober Companion in early 2017.

What's a Recovery Coach/Sober Companion?

"Recovery Coaches/Sober Companions help clients find ways to stop addiction (abstinence) or reduce harm associated with addictive behaviors. These coaches can help a client find resources for harm reduction, detox, treatment, family support and education, local or online support groups; or help a client create a change plan to recover on their own."

My definition?

I get paid a large sum of money to babysit the ultra rich because they're too smart and too wealthy to ever to get sober.

As of this writing, not a single client of mine is sober (or active in recovery).

They refuse to take a look at themselves, and they take the easy way out of everything, which often includes high-end rehab stays and hiring people, like me, to justify the cost.

If the cost is high, then the service must be worth it, right?

That's how some rich people think.

Hiring a Recovery Coach or Sober Companion is super convenient for them.

We're coming to *them*.

The client never has to leave the comfort of their home (or their $5000 a night hotel suite).

And the whole harm reduction part of the definition is something I'll never get my head around. I believe true sobriety is complete abstinence from anything that chemically alters the state of the brain.

I've seen contracts between the client and the company that clearly states that harm reduction is allowed, meaning Johnny or Jane can drink, snort, sniff or ingest any substance under the sun, as long as it's not the substance they have an "issue" with.

I've had clients take Zoloft, Ketamine, and Trazodone, smoke pot, drink and do cocaine, but that's okay, because they're not shooting heroin or popping Oxycontin.

I'll wait while you digest that.

Shall we continue?

That's how fucking twisted (but let's not for get profitable) the addiction industry can be.

But I didn't learn how warped the business is until I was in it.

I went into my first assignment thinking I was going to save the world.

I had every intention of taking my client to 12 step meetings, introducing him to proper diet and exercise, and being a shoulder to cry on.

It didn't work out that way.

I'm not going to get into the specifics, but every single one of my clients had zero desire to get sober.

The millions of dollars the families spent on rehabs and therapists didn't work.

But surely a Recovery Coach/Sober Companion would. Right?

Jay will be living with us. It'll be impossible for Johnny to drink if Jay is here. Right?

Wrong.

I can't keep anyone sober.

Addicts have to *want* it.

None of the clients I've worked with have wanted it. They're just going along with it to appease the family or the boss or the studio executive.

I need to be honest when I say that it was exciting in the beginning, however.

I was living like a millionaire (or sometimes a billionaire).

It was almost impossible *not* to become enchanted by it all.

But it got very old, very quickly.

The excess (in almost every form imaginable) was such a turnoff, not to mention disgusting.

I was raised never to waste anything, to finish everything on my plate, and to make damn good and sure that I turned off the lights every time I walked out of a room.

I've had clients throw thousands of dollars of clothes away (not donated, but tossed in the trash), buy several cars to piss the salesman off (that sit under tarps in the garage) and get entrees from several restaurants because they were in the mood for sushi from this place but wanted chicken livers from that place (throwing away most of it after a bite or two).

One client had a watch collection that exceeded the million dollar mark.

Another had a sports car valued at over $200,000. His girlfriend bought for him. Her family was also the one paying for my Sober Companion services.

A third was upset that he had to wait in a hospital waiting room for twenty minutes, telling me he practically owned the hospital and couldn't believe he had to wait with "these people."

He was also kind enough to tell me, "One isn't a writer simply because one wrote just one book," after I gave him a signed copy of the book you're holding in your hands.

Some people are so insecure they only feel better about themselves when they knock others down.

Oh well.

That's on them.

I feel bad for them.

Money can buy a lot of things, but it doesn't buy manners, morals or class.

And I have zero issue with success.

Nor do I have an issue with people struggling with addiction-obviously.

What I *do* have an issue with, is wealthy people trying to *buy* their way into sobriety.

It doesn't work that way.

It's important to go through the mental, physical and emotional pain we go through when we're new to recovery.

We're supposed to be raw and scared.

We're supposed to be feeling those feelings.

We're not supposed to be running away from them with alternative drugs and harm reduction. All that stuff numbs us and prevents us from getting to the root of what our issues are.

Feeling the pain and shame and guilt is an essential reminder of why it's so important not to want to go back to that lifestyle again.

All of these services my clients pay for *isn't* recovery.

But Recovery Coaching/Sober Companionship is the next "big thing" in the industry.

After Brittany Spears had a meltdown and shaved her head about twelve years ago, companions have been slowly making their way into the mainstream.

Famous people with prior addiction issues sometimes have a Sober Companion written into their film or television contracts, for liability purposes.

Recovery Coaches/Sober Companions don't need any schooling or education either.

It's a two-day online course.

I think my patience and acceptance is far more valuable than a certificate, but that's *only* because of what I've been taught in the 12-step program I belong to.

I continually live what I was taught.

I don't just talk the talk. I walk the walk.

But again, although I can lead by example, I can't force my opinions, beliefs or behavior on anyone.

Besides, most of my clients don't want me there.

I have to shadow them all day, including following them into the bathroom to make sure they don't drink or use.

I wouldn't want me there either.

I struggled with the entire scene at the beginning.

I didn't see my purpose.

I wasn't doing much of anything, other than living their lives with them.

Unsolicited advice is not allowed.

I'm not allowed to talk about the client with other family members.

And rich people don't do much of anything.

Ever.

Considering the resources they have at their fingertips, it's astounding at how often we'd sit around, day after day, doing absolutely nothing.

And without a set agenda or even an end date on some cases, the uncertainty of each assignment can be mentally exhausting, never mind how draining it can be to live with an active addict.

When I talked to a few people in my sober circle about how I was struggling with the entire essence of sober companionship, they told me that I needed to separate my recovery from the job.

So I did.

I no longer have visions of grandeur, thinking I'm going to save my clients.

Now I do my job, and I do it well.

Is it something I want to do forever?

Nope.

I know that much.

I'd much rather work with people who *want* to get sober.

Chapter 17

Nine years ago I gave up *one* thing to have *everything*.

It wasn't easy, but it was worth it.

I don't know much of what the future holds (and I have no control over it anyway).

And that's okay.

I still have no idea what I want to be when I grow up.

I've been looking into college courses lately.

I wrote a book based on my Uber tales, and I've been shopping it around (without success) for the past two years.

I'm also writing a collaboration with a female friend about dating in the dating app world.

I've started a collection of short stories that have the potential to be a stand-alone novel.

It takes place at the lake, or more specifically, the part of the lake I spent with Elle and Grace when I was a couple of years sober.

It was just the Golden Girls and me for an entire month, and it was one of the most important parts of my recovery.

Coincidence that alcoholism touches each

main character in each separate story?

I don't believe in coincidences.

But I'll keep writing because it's what I'm passionate about.

I'll keep going to meetings too.

And I'll keep reaching out to help other addicts who want help.

Beyond that?

Who knows?

But in the meantime, I think I'll take the advice of a sign I saw when I walked into a basement room a few years ago, a room that was far too bright, and smelled of burnt coffee and stale cigarette smoke.

I had nothing inside of me back then, not even hope.

That had been gone for years.

But I *did* have a little willingness.

And that willingness was *just* enough for me to ask for help.

The sign may as well have been written in Greek because it didn't make sense back then.

But it does today.

One Day At A Time.

Epilogue

It's a cold night, in the 40's, but crisp, like most late October nights in New England.

The hall is only half full.

The Sox are in the race for The World Series, and most people are home, watching from the warmth of their living rooms.

A gentleman in his 50's walks to the podium in front, bows his head for a few seconds.

He knows, like most in attendance, that what he's about to say isn't revolutionary, nor is it profound.

And it's been said in a million other meetings, in a thousand other parts of the world.

But what he says is true, and that's what matters.

He talks about what brought him to his knees, talks about how he walked out of the darkness, one step at a time.

Another man listens from the audience, hair receding, whiskers in his scruff more gray than brown.

When his name is called, he walks to the podium.

He hugs the older man, tells him he loves him, and turns to the room.

What he says doesn't matter.

What matters is that there may be another alcoholic there, one who is as hopeless as the man at the podium once was.

And maybe he'll be able to identify with what the man says.

Maybe.

And that's what matters.

Jay Keefe
November 20th, 2018

Acknowledgments

Saying thanks to people at the end of a book is weird.

No one knows the people being thanked except for the people I'm thanking, so it's odd.

Anyway, here goes:

To Dennis: Thank you for reaching out via Facebook and offering your assistance without even knowing me (in person, at least). Your advice, guidance, and answers to my never-ending questions were lifesavers.

To my recovery tribe: You are as much my family as my real clan. And you know who you are. I don't want to waste half a tree naming you all individually, so I won't. Besides, it's an anonymous program.

To my family: Thank you for being patient when I had to remove myself from every major holiday and family event for the first few years of my sobriety.

One time towards my final downward spiral, dad and I were sitting at the picnic table at the lake, and he knew I was hurting.

He looked at the cottage, pointed, and said,

"The best friends you're ever going to have are in that house. Don't be afraid to lean on us."

He was right.

And I did.

Big time.

So, once again, thank you for being my undying support team. Love you guys.

To Brian: I've been in the darkness, and it sucks, and it's scary, and it's lonely, but I promise you, there's a way out. I'll always be here, any time you need me.

Because brothers don't let each other wander in the dark alone.

To Elle: I know you can't read and that some people may think it's insane to thank a dog in a book, but I don't care.

Your love and affection have always been unbreakable and the fact that you greet me at the door like I've been gone for ten years when it's only been ten minutes, means the world to me.

You make me smile and bring me peace every second we're together. If only the rest of us lived in the moment as you do, I think the world would be a better place.

To Grace: No goodbyes monkey. None. I'll see you soon enough. I promise. Wait for me. I'm bringing a Ball-E with me. Or a hundred. Huge to the sky Gracie Girl. Huge to the sky.

To Rae, Liz, and Joey: You've taught me more about *not* sweating the small stuff than anyone I've known.

Rae: Although you're twenty years younger, you'll always be the smarter and more responsible one.

Liz: To have such enormous talent in such a small package is mind-blowing. But it's what's on the inside that counts. And what's in your heart and mind could light the way for a thousand worlds. Keep doing what you're doing, because I, for one, am in awe of you.

Joey: You're one of the good ones. I'll just leave it at that. But trust me, I've only said that about a handful of people. Ask your mom what I mean. She'll be able to explain it much more eloquently than I ever could.

And although I'm now just a silent observer watching from the sidelines, I can't ever possibly express in words how proud I am of each of you.

But I will say this kiddos-huge to the sky.

To my higher power: Who/what/wherever you are, I have two words I hope can begin to convey what you've meant to me over the past nine years:

Endless gratitude.

And yes, I know you've been there all along.

But sometimes it takes me a little while to get out of my own way.

A.A. World Services, Inc.

P.O. Box 459,

Grand Central Station

New York, NY 10163

(212) 870-3400

Made in the
USA
Middletown, DE